Canoe Camping

Canoe Camping

AN INTRODUCTORY GUIDE

By Cecil Kuhne

LYONS & BURFORD, PUBLISHERS

To my parents,
with gratitude

Lyons & Burford
31 West 21 Street
New York, NY 10010

Printed in the United States of America
Design by Joel Friedlander Publishing Services
Photographs by Cecil Kuhne
Illustrations by Cherie Kuhne
10 9 8 7 6 5 4 3 2 1

Library of Congress Cataloging-in-Publication Data
Kuhne, Cecil, 1952–
    Canoe camping: an introductory guide / by Cecil Kuhne.
        p. cm.
    Includes bibliographical references (p.   ).
    ISBN 1-55821-531-X (pbk.)
    1. Canoe camping. I. Title.
GV790.K84 1997
797.1'22—dc21   96-54046
                                              CIP

Contents

Acknowledgments

My thanks go to a number of individuals for their support of this work. I greatly appreciate the assistance of publisher Peter Burford for his endorsement of yet another project. And to Lilly Golden—a writer's dream come true of the perfect editor—I owe much, not only for her thoroughness and encouragement, but for coming up with the idea in the first place.

Few writers persist without encouragement from magazine editors, and I am fortunate to have worked with the talented individuals at *Canoe & Kayak* magazine—David and Judy Harrison, Paul Temple, Jan Nesset, Nancy Harrison Hill.

Likewise, a paddler doesn't go far without help from his paddling friends, and I consider myself lucky indeed to count as friends many of the staff members at Nantahala Outdoor Center, with whom I hope to be swinging a paddle for a long time.

Lastly, I owe a huge debt of gratitude to my wife, Cherie, a constant river companion and the one whose skillful drawings grace the pages of this book.

Introduction:
The Perfect Campsite

Even in well-traveled canoeing circles, the river wasn't well known. After pulling out a thick, expensive atlas only to discover that it didn't even have a map of the area, my wife and I knew we were in for something just a little remote.

Canada's North Country evokes the stereotypical images—husky-powered sled teams, rustic Hudson's Bay Trading Posts, and of course stern Canadian Mounties. Here still exist places where no roads lead and no jetliners land. One such place is Nahanni. Nestled next to the Yukon in a secluded corner of the vast Northwest Territories, this pocket of pristine backcountry is abruptly bisected by the broad and powerful waters of the South Nahanni River. It was our dream to spend two weeks paddling down this untamed river, and the seemingly unattainable idea eventually became a reality. The river, in the end, exceeded our highest expectations.

The Nahanni has everything a canoeist longs for—big flows, exciting rapids, easy hikes to alpine lakes, abundant wildlife (bears, caribou, foxes, moose, and bighorn sheep), a waterfall twice the height of Niagara, and just incidentally some of the most splendid campsites on the planet.

Any journey by canoe into the wilderness is a passage from one life to another. You leave the noisy and predictable routine of the city for the quietude and uncertainty of nature. The deeper you paddle into this world, the more your perspective will change. You will see new things, of course, but you will hear, smell, and feel them with an intensity you never thought possible.

These indelible impressions become imprinted on the mind. At the fast pace of my life in a big metropolis, I sometimes can't remember things that happened that morning. Yet images of canoe trips I took a decade ago are so crystal clear it seems as if they happened yesterday. Especially memorable are the glorious campsites we pitched on those long, pleasant journeys downstream.

I vividly recall an alpine lake whose banks seemed to heave straight up toward the heavens. Sunshine streamed into the narrow gorge to warm the white beaches spotted with lichen-stained rocks. Side canyons, filled with ferns and berry bushes, occasionally pierced the chasm to allow creeks to flow through. Along the shore lived deer, elk, bighorn sheep, and mountain goats. Almost every day we spotted otters, martens, kingfishers, and herons. High above flew ospreys and bald eagles.

I remember paddling between the windswept ridges and crags of a desert stream. There the gentle flow of the river piled itself against precipitous cliffs, where light danced upon the swirling surface. The air was as dry and brittle as the canyon walls that etched the cobalt sky. You could feel on your face the gentle, unceasing wind. The silence there was profound. At night we gazed up at that narrow swath at the top of the canyon—and into a pitch-black, star-filled sky—and the rest of the world seemed very far away indeed.

I'll never forget a canoe trip through the jagged plateau known as the Ozarks. It was a place of dense forest, steep valleys, imposing bluffs, mysterious caves, and most impressive of all—clear, rushing springs. Spewing from the earth, these cascades were amazing not only for their limitless abundance, but for their perfect purity. As they chattered noisily over polished boulders, the rivulets joined together to become a pulsing, living force. This was a river lounger's dream come true: Opposite every bluff, it seemed, was a wide, pebbled beach perfect for camping.

On most of these canoe camping trips, my companions and I spent only five or six hours a day on the water. In the campsites we pitched along the way, there was always plenty of time for other diversions—fly fishing, photography, a little wildlife observation, perhaps a brisk day hike, even a relaxing soak in hot springs. We kept asking the same rhetorical question: Does a mortal's life get any better than this?

The camaraderie that developed among us on these wilderness wanderings was especially memorable. Spending long days sharing adventures in spectacular surroundings has a way of bringing people close together. Even now, we refer to trips that occurred so many years ago.

The notion of packing up your gear for a weeklong camping trip is a seemingly simple one: Assemble your things, pile them into a canoe, and head out. But there is more here than meets the eye. My favorite wilderness author, Sigurd Olson, describes well the sublime joys of canoe camping—and their subtle impact on the soul:

> There is the feel of a paddle and the movement of a canoe, a magic compounded by distance, adventure, solitude, and peace. The way of a canoe is the way of the wilderness and of a freedom almost forgotten, the open door to waterways of ages past and a way of life with profound and abiding satisfactions.

1

The Touring Boat

THE TRIP BEGAN as we slipped our canoes into the clear, cold waters of the mountain lakes that would be the object of our pursuit for the next several days. The jade green waters were calm and glassy here, and the boats swished their wakes so cleanly across the surface that the water seemed to crack with the intrusion.

On that trip, and others to follow, it became obvious that the canoe is one of those inspired human designs—elegant, efficient, simple, adaptable. It is sleek enough to glide through water with heavy loads; stable in turbulence; capable of holding a straight line in the wind, yet maneuverable in whitewater; light enough to be portaged, but rugged enough to withstand abuse. It is, in short, a creation perfectly suited to its place and purpose.

GENERAL CONSIDERATIONS

A canoe journey, like others, begins in the mind. The idea for a trip develops, and the imagination runs wild with the possibilities. But inevitably the practical considerations must be faced, and the foremost among these is the choice of a boat.

No matter from what angle you look at it, the design of a canoe is impressive. The lines of the boat are not only pleasing to the eye, but incredibly practical for hauling loads that would sink lesser craft. Very few boats of such slender profile can accommodate your camping gear for a week, or more, on a journey piercing deep into the backcountry.

The touring canoe is different from one made for speed or one made for whitewater: It will easily accept your tent, sleeping bags, clothes, food, kitchen utensils, and all the other luxuries that backpackers can only dream about. But not all touring canoes are born alike, and some perform better than others at specific tasks. Naturally, there is friendly debate about which is best.

Almost any washtub will move you downstream, but safety and comfort demand a more sophisticated craft. The ultimate decision is a subjective one, but a few guidelines may prove helpful. Good canoe design is really just a matter of combining the best possible features (with off-putting names such as *freeboard, cross-section shape, sheer line,* and *tumblehome*). There is no such thing as the right design, because each design feature has an influence on all the others. So, in simple terms, what makes for a good touring canoe? Experienced canoeists agree on a few basic principles:

A length of 17 feet is considered the absolute minimum, and many canoeists prefer longer 18- or 18½-foot models.

The canoe should have substantial depth and volume. Larger canoes not only allow for bigger loads but provide a greater margin of safety on rough water.

Most important, you need a good, strong boat for touring. Then, the lighter the boat, the better.

The canoe must be trustworthy and forgiving on all types of water. A reputable manufacturer is the best assurance of a well-made craft.

The major concern is *safety*. The backcountry is no place to experiment with specialized canoes that offer a slight advantage in performance at the expense of strength and predictability.

CAPACITY

The most important variable affecting canoe length is the amount of gear the canoeist intends to carry. So you'll first need to

Canoe livery on the Buffalo River.

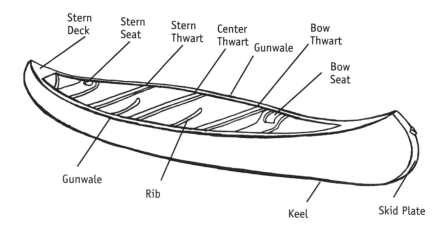

Anatomy of a canoe

sit down and figure out just how much gear you'll have on a typical trip.

Most touring canoeists find that, for all-around tandem use, a high-volume, 17- to 18-foot boat is the best choice. Certainly, shorter boats offer advantages in handling and control, but they're frequently too small to accommodate all the camping gear you'd like to take.

A longer canoe will also ride the waves of a river or a wind-tossed lake more smoothly than a short one. A 15-footer will torque out with each oncoming wave, which leaves you fighting to keep on course. Add a foot more length and you suddenly gain stability and a much better ride. Increase the length to 18 or 18½ feet and the craft becomes completely manageable, rising and falling gently with the waves.

Long canoes may be more manageable than short ones, but they don't always run drier. If the distance between waves is shorter than the canoe's length, the canoe may plow into the waves and take on significant amounts of water. Under these conditions, a shorter canoe—one that fits between the waves—will be drier, though it might make for a rougher ride.

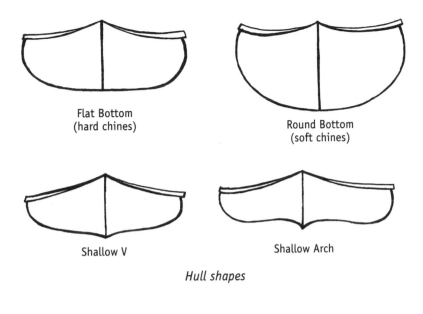

Flat Bottom
(hard chines)

Round Bottom
(soft chines)

Shallow V

Shallow Arch

Hull shapes

DESIGN

Canoeists, if anything, are an opinionated lot. They know what they like to paddle, and they'll be glad to tell you about it. A long evening passed in such conversation will no doubt yield a variety of viewpoints on topics such as stability, water displacement, speed, bow profiles, hull shape, stem shape, and upturn of the bow and stern. But the general principles of canoe design are really quite simple.

You'll learn that hulls with flat bottoms, *hard chines* (a sharp, nearly right-angle edge where bottom and sides meet), and *tumblehome* (curved sides rolling inward at the top) have great initial stability, but next to no secondary stability. In other words, it takes some effort to start them tipping, but once on their way, they're gone. Conversely, round hulls with *soft chines* (a gradual curve where bottom and sides meet) and flared sides have much less initial stability, and as a result, they feel "tippy." But once they start to tip over, they show great final stability and they require some indiscretion from you (or a good boost from wind or waves) to capsize them.

You'll learn that a long, skinny canoe with a sharp bow will be fast. This is because it slices through the water rather than bashes into it, thus piling it up in front of the boat. If you make a canoe broad in the beam, and then carry that fullness forward and aft, you'll have a freighter, not a racer. The canoe may be great for carrying big loads and riding waves, but it will not be quick.

Most canoes fall somewhere in between. Canoes designed for backcountry travel are asked to do just about everything—carry big loads, endure heavy waves, maintain directional stability, maneuver through whitewater, and yet remain relatively easy and fast to paddle. They'll be long enough (17 to 18½ feet) to remain fairly narrow even with a beam of 34 to 36 inches. Entry lines will be slim enough to ease paddling, but then flare at the quarters to improve buoyancy and load-bearing capacity. There will be some *rocker* (upward curve in the keel line) to let the boat turn and spin easily, yet not so much that the canoe is impossible to hold on course when crossing a breezy lake.

Entire books have been written on the subject of canoe design, and much of the material is quite technical. Needless to say, a discussion of the esoteric advantages of various canoe designs—along with its technical nomenclature—is beyond the scope of a book on canoe camping. Good references for further study in this area are *The Canoe Handbook,* by Slim Ray, and *Canoeing: The Complete Guide to Equipment and Technique,* by Dave Harrison. Also helpful is a knowledgeable canoe dealer you can speak with personally.

Perhaps better yet is an association with a canoe club where you can meet others who have paddled various models and who will let you try a hand at paddling their boats. There's nothing like an on-the-water test to determine how you like a particular model. At the very least, you should rent before you buy—it's too big an investment to do otherwise.

MATERIALS

The list of materials from which canoes are built is expanding at a mind-numbing pace, and the choices can be intimidating. A

canoe designer looks for a material that balances three elements—
weight, strength, and cost—in a way that matches a clear vision of
how the boat should perform.

Let's start with weight. The lighter the boat, the less water it
has to displace as it moves through the water. Often, however,
weight is reduced at the expense of durability.

With exotic materials, designers can produce a hull that is
exceptionally strong and light, but the cost is usually prohibitive.
Strong hulls can be made from less expensive materials, but this
usually means a heavier boat. If the canoe is designed for river use,
where the current does most of the work and the longest portage is
from the car to the put-in, the extra weight may be acceptable. But
if you're dealing with lakes or frequent portages, a lighter canoe
makes more sense.

One way designers balance weight, strength, and cost is by rein-
forcing only those parts that receive the most stress. The ends and
bottom of a hull take the most abuse from impact and abrasion, so
additional material is placed there. The key is to decide how much
(and where) additional material is needed to make the hull stiff
enough to resist bending, yet flexible enough to distribute stress.

Sometimes a designer has only one logical choice of material
for a given design, while other models can be offered in two or three
different materials. Don't let a certain material keep you from considering a particular canoe, and don't buy a more expensive material than you need. Choose the balance of weight, strength, and cost
that matches your idea of what you want your boat to do. Remember, you're buying a boat, not a material.

Most boats manufactured today are made of plastic, composite, aluminum, or wood; here's a brief introduction to each:

Plastics

Not all plastics are alike, and there are considerable differences
among them in terms of strength, weight, performance, and maintenance.

ROYALEX.

This plastic consists of a foam core sandwiched between sheets
of ABS (Acrylonitrile Butadiene Styrene) with layers of vinyl on

top. It's extremely tough: an obvious choice for whitewater and general recreation canoes when durability is important. Royalex requires little maintenance, is relatively easy to repair (though rarely needs it), and is moderately priced. For all these reasons it's one of the most popular materials.

MOLDED POLYETHYLENE.

Polyethylene is inexpensive, durable, slips easily over rocks, and can be molded into complex shapes. There are two common types: linear and cross-linked. Strands of linear polyethylene are very long, while cross-linked strands are shorter and chemically bonded to one another. Linear is easier to recycle, cross-linked is stiffer.

To make a hull, manufacturers use two processes: roto-molding and blow-molding. The most perceptible difference is that a blow-molded hull is thicker, heavier, and stiffer. Some manufacturers combine roto-molded polyethylene and foam into a plastic-foam laminate.

Composites

These canoes are made by fitting layers of cloth into a mold and adding resin to create a stiff, tough shell. The most common fabrics are fiberglass and the more durable Kevlar, but composites also include materials such as graphite.

A good fiberglass boat can be very tough, though sometimes not durable enough for repeated whitewater use. A *chopper gun lay-up boat* (which refers to the process of mixing chopped-glass fibers with resin and spraying it into a mold, gradually building up the hull) is usually less expensive than one made of cloth; it can be durable, but quality varies widely.

A Kevlar boat ends up weighing about 25 percent less than its fiberglass counterpart, yet with added strength. Fiberglass and Kevlar can be combined in a variety of configurations. All these materials allow builders to create complex shapes with sharp, efficient lines. The sophistication of these materials is reflected in their high prices.

Most composite hulls have an outer layer of gel-coat resin, which protects the fabric from sunlight and abrasion and gives the hull its color and shine. Gel-coat can add up to 10 pounds to the weight of the boat.

Aluminum

The aluminum canoe arose from World War II technology and effectively ended the wood-and-canvas era. Aluminum offered lighter weight, lower cost, no maintenance, and remarkable durability. There are, however, criticisms: It sticks when scraping over rocks, it radiates heat and cold, it transmits noise, and it lacks aesthetics.

Aluminum hulls are made by stretching two metal sheets over a mold, then joining them with rivets along the keel and ends. End caps, thwarts, seats, and gunwales are then riveted into place, and aluminum ribs are spot-welded to stiffen the hull.

Wood and Canvas

The wood-and-canvas builder steams the ribs of the canoe to make them flexible and sets them into place over a metal form. Cedar planking is then attached to the ribs with copper nails. Canvas is stretched over the hull and covered with filler to provide a smooth surface. The outside of the hull receives several coats of paint for a watertight finish, the remaining trim is added, and the wood is varnished. Beautiful to behold (and expensive), wood-and-canvas canoes require constant maintenance to keep in their original condition.

Wood and Fiberglass

Commonly called strippers, these canoes have long, thin planks of wood (usually cedar or redwood) that are glued together without ribs. The hull is then covered inside and out with fiberglass cloth and resin. The strips can be molded into highly complex shapes, and the hull may be very lightweight. These boats are attractive, but also expensive and less durable than those made of plastics or composites.

All Wood

These canoes are beautiful, and most are lapstrake or birchbark. With lapstrakes, cedar planking is nailed to ribs; the planks overlap like clapboard siding on a house, or they can be beveled and fitted to create a smooth exterior. The birchbark canoe is the original boat of the Native North Americans, and only a few are now made by those who have studied the age-old craft.

Folding Canoes

These folding craft have a fabric skin of coated nylon that is stretched over a wood or aluminum frame. Folding canoes and kayaks have been around since the turn of the century, and the longevity of the concept is a testament to their durability. Disassembled, the whole boat fits into two or three duffels that can be checked as luggage or stored in a closet. These craft are slightly less responsive than hard-shell canoes, and they can be expensive.

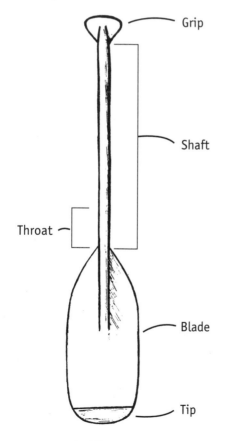

Paddle anatomy

Grip

Shaft

Throat

Blade

Tip

PADDLES

A good touring paddle should be strong, light, and well balanced. The choice is not as easy as it would first appear—which design, which material, which size? And yet the decision is an important one: After hundreds, even thousands, of paddling strokes a day, the wrong choice will be only too evident to your arm and back muscles.

Design

Canoe paddle designs can be almost as specialized as canoes. The most basic blade shape is a rectangular one, but the trend in recent years has been toward smaller, faster blades with a so-called "tulip" shape. Also popular is the long, narrow beavertail design, which is excellent for subtle steering maneuvers. A bent-shaft paddle, which has its blade set at an angle to its shaft, allows for a more efficient stroke because the blade stays vertical until almost the end of the stroke.

Large blades are based on the theory that the more water you move, the more power. But most canoeists now believe that a strong stroke is a matter of blade control, not size. A slightly smaller blade is preferable if you anticipate a lot of flat water or wind. A blade with a rounded end will enter the water more cleanly.

Bent-shaft paddles are great for propulsion, and they provide better control than straight-shaft models. But the bent-shaft is designed to use the same face for all paddling strokes, so reversing the blade (as in certain maneuvers, such as a low brace) is awkward.

The grip of a paddle is also important because it's where most of the control comes from. Many paddlers prefer a T-shaped grip because it provides greater control, but the pear-shaped grip is favored by others for its comfortable feel.

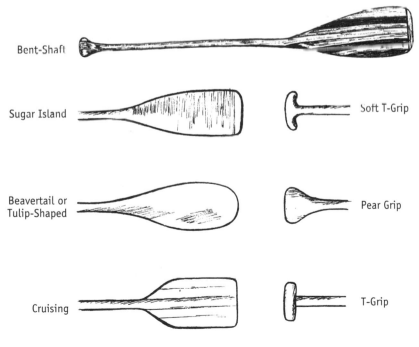

Bent-Shaft

Sugar Island   Soft T-Grip

Beavertail or
Tulip-Shaped   Pear Grip

Cruising   T-Grip

Paddle shapes

Materials

Paddles are made of various materials and each differs in feel, weight, and durability. There is a lively debate among canoeists about which is the most desirable.

WOOD.

Most wooden paddles are made from strips of wood glued or laminated together. Sitka spruce, western red cedar, and ash are common. Many of the better models are covered with a protective layer of fiberglass, while others are finished with varnish. Tips are often reinforced with hardwood or fiberglass, or capped with metal or plastic.

Wood, while beautiful, is expensive and requires frequent care. Wooden paddles, even those from the same manufacturer, may vary considerably in weight, balance, and beauty. But many paddlers feel their pleasing flexibility can't be duplicated in a synthetic material.

SYNTHETICS.

Fabrics such as Kevlar, graphite, and carbon fiber are light and strong, but they're expensive. Fiberglass occupies the middle ground in price, weight, durability, and aesthetics. There are some surprisingly good, yet inexpensive, paddles made with fiberglass blades and aluminum shafts. Other paddles are made completely out of ABS plastic, and the shaft and blade are molded together; these are durable and inexpensive, but often very heavy.

Weight is important, but how it's distributed makes a big difference in the "feel" of the paddle. Some paddlers prefer a thicker blade: They seem to "stick" to the water. Others like a thin blade, which feels faster.

Size

Most canoe paddles, if placed upright, should extend somewhere between your chest and shoulders. The stern paddler might want one an inch or two longer than the bow paddler, who finds a shorter paddle easier to swing from one side to the other.

You'll want a paddle long enough to allow you to reach the water and get good leverage, yet short enough so that you can move it quickly. The shorter the paddle, the more you'll have to compensate with your body to reach. Skill level makes a difference: An experienced paddler can get more leverage with a shorter paddle.

If you're an average-sized person paddling an average-sized canoe with a straight-shaft paddle, you probably can't go wrong with a 56- to 58-inch paddle. If you want a bent-shaft paddle, you might start with a 52-inch paddle. The choice is eventually a subjective one, so try various lengths before you buy.

PACKING THE CANOE

Efficient packing begins with checklists (see the appendices for samples). After several trips, you'll no doubt develop your own. Carefully going through one is the best—and only—way to make certain nothing is forgotten or left behind. A trip can be ruined if someone shows up at the put-in of a wild river without a life jacket, or if everyone arrives in camp to discover that no one remembered to bring matches.

How gear fits into the canoe depends on the individual boat and the preferences of the canoeist loading it. In general, though, you'll want to put as much of your gear as possible into one large waterproof bag (see the discussion on waterproof bags in chapter 9). One bag will hold more than several smaller ones, and there's the added advantage of having only one waterproof seal to worry about. It's also easier to secure a single bag to the boat.

The drawback is finding that certain item you happen to need at the moment. To prevent this frustration, try to pack with unloading in mind: Place toward the *bottom* of the bag those camp items (such as the tent and sleeping bag) you'll need that evening, and toward the *top* of the bag the warm clothing or rain gear you'll need during the day. Many canoeists carry a smaller "day bag" where they can stow clothing and other items they'll want before camp—camera, sunglasses, suntan lotion, gloves, and so forth. Keep a water container handy, too.

When you pack the canoe for the first time, or if you're trying a different load, test it at home first to make sure everything fits. It's frustrating to arrive at the water and discover either that half your gear won't fit, or that you left behind something that would have fit after all.

To properly rig a canoe with camping gear, keep the heavy items low and in the middle of the boat. With most items in one large bag, this is easier. Before you tie down the load and head out, take a short test run. If it doesn't feel right, paddle back to shore, rearrange it, then try again. Have another paddler check the waterline of your boat. Before you hit the water, you'll want everything in order.

Packed for a week's trip into the wilds.

When securing their loads, many canoeists prefer straps and bungee cords instead of ropes. With straps, you don't have to remember knots. Straps are easier to unfasten, and they cinch down tighter with less effort. But for many canoeists, knots are an integral part of canoeing lore, and there's added satisfaction in how many knots you can tie from memory. The recommended resource on this topic is *The Book of Outdoor Knots,* by Peter Owen.

Always tie or strap in *everything.* That way, nothing will be lost, even if the boat capsizes. And don't leave any loose ends of ropes or webbing that could entangle you should the boat overturn.

PORTAGING

There comes a time in every canoeist's life when the inevitable must be faced—the portage, the task of carrying the canoe over land rather than floating it down a certain section of water. Whether you need to avoid an obstacle such as a stretch of whitewater or you simply need to move the canoe to the next lake, the techniques of portaging the boat and gear are essentially the same. Most canoeists find that a canoe is best carried by two people who hoist the empty boat upside down onto their shoulders. The canoe can rest on their shoulders, or they can tuck their heads inside the canoe, supporting their hands on the gunwales.

The best method is for the canoeist in front to stay outside the boat for better visibility, while the rear canoeist keeps his or her head inside the boat for stability. Attaching paddles to the thwarts to make a portage yoke on which you can rest your shoulders is recommended. Using padding or a specially made yoke provides more comfort for your shoulders.

After the canoe is moved, then the rest of the camping and other gear can be carried. Most boaters move the canoe a few hundred yards and then put it down and retrieve the gear. This method gives you a chance to rest from hauling a heavy boat. On trips with a number of canoeists, it's possible to move a canoe across a short portage without having to empty it; the loaded boat is simply hoisted on a number of able shoulders.

PADDLING TECHNIQUE

The intricacies of canoeing strokes, safety procedures, and reading whitewater are beyond the scope of a book on canoe camping, and deserving of a book of their own. Fortunately for canoeists, there are a number of excellent ones available. Especially helpful is Bill Mason's classic, *Path of the Paddle*. Also recommended are Dave Harrison's *Canoeing: The Complete Guide to Equipment and Technique* and Slim Ray's *The Canoe Handbook*. For beginning canoeists, there's *Canoeing Made Easy,* by I. Herbert Gordon, and *Canoeing Basics,* by Melinda Allan.

For an in-depth study of safety and rescue methods, canoeists can do no better than *River Rescue,* by Les Bechdel and Slim Ray, and *Whitewater Rescue Manual,* by Charles Walbridge and Wayne Sundmacher.

Once you've acquired a boat and the necessary skills for handling it, you're now ready to begin that glorious, long-awaited camping trip into the Back of Beyond.

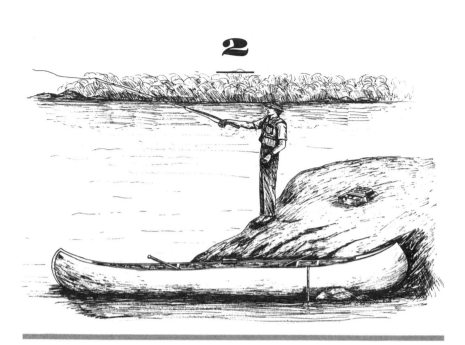

Planning the Trip

THE PADDLING TRIP had been planned for months, and we would soon be leaving on a two-week journey through the Boundary Waters. The last-minute details remained, as they always do, but the trip would ultimately justify our efforts—as it always does.

THE MASTER PLAN

A canoe camping trip naturally involves a great deal of planning and provisioning in order for things to go smoothly. Before making your sojourn into the wild, you'll need to:

- Assemble a group of paddlers
- Consult guidebooks for details about the rivers or lakes you have in mind
- Pick a suitable river or lake based on season, access points, rapids, etc.
- Gather additional information from local boaters or outfitters
- Call government agencies to see if permits are required
- Acquire any river or camping permits and fishing licenses you may need
- Check additional government regulations (regarding required equipment such as portable toilets, firepans, first-aid kits, etc.)
- Arrange and plan shuttles
- Plan menus
- Check basic gear list
- Check safety/rescue gear list
- Check camping and cooking gear lists
- Buy or rent any missing items or gear
- Check water levels of the river or lake
- Check the weather forecast
- Check the difficulty of the river or crossing
- Make certain that portions of the river or crossing are not too dangerous to paddle

It's an intimidating list at first glance, but most canoeists actually find that plotting and then anticipating the journey is half the fun.

Fortunately, a great wealth of information exists on canoeing destinations. Guidebooks have been published about hundreds of rivers, lakes, and bayous throughout the United States. Some of these concentrate on a specific spot, while others describe a number of trips within a geographical region.

Topographic maps may also be useful to show the surrounding land features and potential places to camp. Some government agencies can provide camping information on the particular areas they manage. Maps designed for canoeists usually have suggestions on campsites.

Don't forget public libraries. Many now have an interlibrary loan system that allows you to request almost any book or map published. Other sources of information worth gathering include members of boating clubs or knowledgeable employees at canoe shops. Now there's even the Internet, with Web groups and bulletin boards dedicated specifically to canoeing.

Seasons

After you decide *where* to go, you'll need to decide *when* to go. Peak runoff is the time when rivers have their highest flows. In dry years, the peak may not mean much, but it usually means high water, often running at dangerous levels. As a result, the river courses through trees and bushes, places to stop are few, there's less time to make decisions, the powerful current is less forgiving, and the water temperature is cold.

On smaller rivers, the peak may only last a few days, and the river eventually drops to a point where it's too low to run. This commonly happens on rivers in the eastern United States or small rivers with relatively dry drainage areas. On these rivers, the season is limited to a few months in the spring or the days following a rainstorm. In the western United States, larger rivers usually have a big peak, then drop slowly throughout the summer.

The challenge on smaller rivers with short seasons is to learn the optimum times. Good guidebooks often supply this information, but the best source is boaters who run the river often.

Water Flow

The amount of water flowing down a river is typically measured in cubic feet per second (or cubic meters per second). This data is collected by various government agencies, and good guidebooks indicate which levels are best for canoeing.

Information on river levels is becoming readily accessible. Many newspapers publish flows of local rivers, and hot lines with recorded flow messages are available. For phone numbers or flow information, check with whitewater shops and government agencies managing the river. If the river lies below a dam, call the agency managing the dam and ask about releases. Information can sometimes be obtained from state offices of the U.S. Geological Survey and the National Weather Service.

Hydrographs showing the flow each month for an average year are sometimes available from governmental sources. These are especially useful to canoeists in their long-term planning.

INITIAL PLANNING

The initial planning for a canoe journey starts with the seed of an idea. Eventually that dream blossoms into a full-blown trip, with all the planning and provisioning that such an endeavor entails. A number of decisions will have to be made along the way, the first of which is how luxuriously you wish to travel.

Camping Styles

Camping styles vary. Equipment on luxury canoe trips consists of just about anything you can take on a car camping trip. Large tents, bulky sleeping bags, and even cots can be carried. Big stoves with propane tanks may be appropriate for large groups. Meals on these trips are often elaborate affairs. Fresh vegetables, fruits, and meats are packed in coolers, and cooking can be done in the heaviest of cast-iron ovens and pans. Some canoeists even take lawn chairs for relaxing by the water, while others pack volleyball sets.

The equipment you pack will depend on the style you choose. Obviously, luxurious trips with fresh food and mounds of equipment require more extensive planning.

Longer Trips

Longer canoe trips—spanning more than a weekend—naturally involve more advance planning. Some require preparation weeks, even months, in advance. Because such trips demand more preparation, let's take a close look at them.

REGULATED RIVERS.

Some areas have become so popular that the number of boaters is causing environmental damage: Vegetation is trampled, campfire scars abound, and disposal of human waste presents sanitation problems.

To minimize this impact, some government agencies have developed regulations to protect the resource, including the requirement that you apply in advance for a permit to run the river or camp along the lake (often a lottery is held). You'll want to write ahead of time: Six months to a year isn't too early for the most popular sites. Information about permits is found in most guidebooks and sourcebooks.

ASSEMBLING THE PARTY.

A canoeing group can range from one friend to a dozen or more companions. Smaller groups involve fewer planning hassles, and in many cases, there's less damage to the environment. Some areas managed by government agencies may require you to keep the party within a certain size. Regardless of the group, everyone should be sufficiently experienced for the trip you're about to undertake.

DISPERSING INFORMATION.

Get your party together far in advance of the trip. Talk over dates, equipment, costs, and so on. Delegate duties, and put someone in charge of renting or borrowing additional boats and assembling other group gear.

PREPARATION DAY.

Some canoe parties tack on an extra day at the beginning of the trip to spend time in town buying food, packing vehicles, and so forth.

LENGTH OF TRIP.

Find out how long it normally takes to make the trip and adapt this to your plans. Give yourself plenty of leeway. The actual time will depend on many factors, such as how high the water is, the direction of the winds, and the number of portages.

Trip Costs

Trip expenses may be fairly simple for small groups, or they may become complicated, as when a twelve-member group embarks on a two-week trip into a remote wilderness. For efficiency, groups usually pool their money. Before proceeding too far in the planning, it's best to make a cost estimate:

- How many vehicles will be used? What's the distance from your home to the destination and back? What's the distance involved in the shuttle? From this total mileage, you can estimate your gas costs.
- If you use the services of a commercial shuttle driver, add that expense.
- Based on the number of people in your group, estimate the cost of food for the trip.
- Add any expenses of renting equipment.
- Estimate costs of group supplies, such as stove fuel, batteries, charcoal briquettes, etc.

With all this in mind, figure up the total sum and then add a margin of error. Always ask for more than you need: At the end of a trip it's easy to refund money, but if you spend more than you have, it's sometimes unpleasant to collect the amount of your shortage.

It may be a good idea to ask for a deposit early in the planning process. This will give you an idea of how many people are going: When people put their money down, it makes their commitment more serious.

GROUP DYNAMICS

For longer trips, the number of people planning to go will no doubt change. Vacation schedules change, someone gets ill, and a host of other circumstances can alter the list. You therefore need to make your plans flexible enough to adjust for a different-sized group.

Main Group-Planning Session

At some point, you'll want to get the final group together before the trip. Because of changes that can occur, you may want to have a group meeting a week, or just a few days, before the departure date. With a meeting that close to the departure, you'll have a better idea of exactly how many are going. At this meeting, you can divide the responsibilities for last-minute details.

FOOD.

Planning menus, buying food, and preparing meals can be done in several ways:

- Group members can bring their own food and do their own cooking. This plan is best for small parties, in which one stove or fire can be shared as each person cooks his or her own meal. With larger groups, food is typically bought collectively.

- One or more members of the group can volunteer to do all the menu planning, food buying, and cooking.

- The responsibilities for meals can be divided among the party. Each person is responsible for preparing a specific meal or meals for the group.

COLLECTING MONEY.

At the final meeting, collect the rest of the money. Some of it can be given to those buying food and the rest can be used for gas, assuming equipment rental has been taken care of.

PERSONAL EQUIPMENT.

Go over a list of personal gear and be sure everyone has adequate equipment and clothing for the trip.

EXPECTATIONS AND SAFETY.

From the beginning, it's important that everyone knows he or she will be expected to help. Each day boats will need to be loaded and unloaded, campsites pitched, the kitchen set up, and so on. If everyone is prepared to pitch in, the trip will run more smoothly, and there will be more leisure time. Everyone should also realize there are potential dangers in any wilderness travel. From a legal standpoint, as well as a moral one, make it clear that the trip will not be free from danger. After a review of the hazards, stress the importance of safety.

ENVIRONMENT.

Remind everyone of the appropriate techniques to minimize environmental impact (explained in detail in chapter 4). Remember to use only biodegradable soap and to dispose of garbage properly. Consider the use of firepans to prevent damage to campsites. These and other precautions will help maintain our waterways in a pristine condition.

Leadership

There can be a designated leader on a canoeing trip, but more often than not, a democratic system develops. In certain situations where the group has to make important safety decisions (such as whether to paddle a river in high flows), inexperienced boaters should defer to opinions of the more experienced. As long as everyone maintains an easygoing attitude, things will proceed smoothly.

Safety in Numbers

Traveling with an experienced group is no doubt the safest situation. On really difficult rivers or large lakes, it may be better to organize a party of at least four or five boats so you have extra people to help if trouble occurs. It's especially important to adhere to this rule when you're a beginner.

Occasionally, canoeists prefer to boat alone, realizing that their solitude increases the risks. Although they're going against the traditional wisdom, if they adhere to proper safety precautions veteran boaters can have safe, rewarding experiences on their own.

Children

With careful planning, canoe camping can be enjoyed by the entire family. When you bring children along, there are some important points to keep in mind:

- Choose easy rivers and lakes with little possibility of capsizing a boat.

- Be certain all children know how to swim. Teach your children not to be afraid of water, and start them swimming at an early age.

- Let children help with repairs and general maintenance of the boats.

- Make the first trip a short one; a couple of hours is best.

- Always have children wear life jackets (wear yours to set a good example). Use jackets that will provide good buoyancy and keep a child's head upright in water. Teach children how to fasten their jackets, and be sure there's no way they can slip out of them. Before the trip, have the children swim in a pool with their jackets on.

TRANSPORTATION

If you're planning a lightweight trip, transporting equipment may not present much of a problem. For luxurious trips, getting to and from the river can be a more complex undertaking:

- Cartop racks can be used to carry canoes on the smallest of cars; a sturdy rack can be used for carrying other gear as well.

- Pickup trucks, vans, and other sport-utility vehicles are useful for carrying gear, but be careful not to load them beyond their recommended limits.

- Trailers can be rented or borrowed and are especially helpful for transporting several canoes.

On trips when vehicles are subjected to much wear and tear, you might consider reimbursing the vehicles' owners. It may also be a good idea to caravan in case car trouble develops. One last comment: Be sure everyone knows *exactly* where you're going.

Shuttles

By their nature, river trips start at one point and end at another, so somehow you must shuttle your vehicles. There are a number of ways of accomplishing the chore. This is certainly the most frustrating and time-consuming aspect of any trip, but the easiest solution, no doubt, is to hire a commercial shuttle driver. To find one, contact the nearest chamber of commerce or the government agency managing the river.

You can set up your own shuttles by leaving one vehicle (or more) at each end. This works well if there's not too much distance involved and you have plenty of time. Shuttles can involve an infinite variety of combinations, but the most common are:

- For two vehicles: Drive to the take-out and leave one vehicle there. Then everyone drives to the put-in in the other vehicle.

- For more than two vehicles: Drive to the put-in and unload all the people and gear. Then drive the vehicles to the take-out and leave all but one of them there. Using that one vehicle, return all the drivers to the put-in.

Either way, you'll naturally have to retrieve the vehicle at the put-in after the trip.

In performing a shuttle, make it clear to the others where you've put your car keys. If an accident occurs and help must be summoned, everyone needs to know where the keys are. Some people bring along two sets and keep them in separate boats in case of an upset. Others hide the keys on the vehicle so that the keys and vehicle are together. In some areas, theft of parked cars is a problem, so be sure to hide the keys well. Also, be sure you don't accidentally leave the keys to the *take-out* vehicle at the *put-in* vehicle!

One last note about shuttles and driving. Many consider driving to the destination to be the most dangerous part of a canoe trip, because vehicles are heavily loaded, drivers are sleepy, and everyone is anxious to get on the water. Whenever you drive, use care and caution.

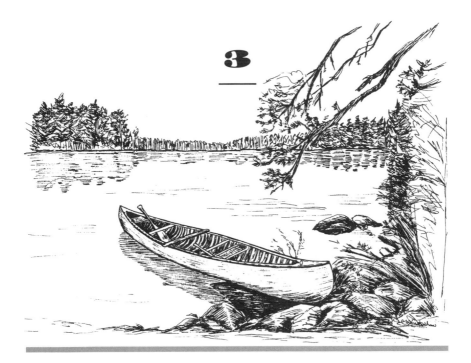

Selecting Campsites

IT WAS SPRING in the South and the dense forest was set ablaze with the vivid blossoms of redbud, rhododendron, azalea, and laurel. The sheer cliffs climbed hundreds of feet above this Ozark stream, where we had pitched our tents on a shimmering gravel bar shaded by the dense canopy of an old sycamore tree. Light danced on the current as it swept by and disappeared around a bend downstream. Life was very good, thanks to a fortunate choice of campsite.

THE IDEAL SITE

Everyone has a notion of the ideal spot in which to pitch a tent for the night. In his book *Broken Waters Sing* veteran river runner Gaylord Staveley describes what he affectionately calls The Perfect Campsite:

> It has a sandy beach long enough for all the boats and is moderately sloping so that their bows slide up on it easily . . . . Only two or three steps up the beach is a dry, level area that camp can be unloaded to, and within reaching distance of the campfire is a large snap of dry driftwood consisting of twigs for tinder, medium limbs for cooking, and heavy chunks for night logs. A clear little creek enters the river at this point. Back away from the beach is a ten- or twenty-acre domain of untracked sand, free of sagebrush and cactus, and gently duned to provide each camper with his own little pocket.

But Staveley doesn't stop there:

> The site has shade when the afternoon is hot and sun when
> the morning is cool. There are no flies, mosquitoes, gnats,
> cattle, or other river parties. The view in any direction is a
> grand composite of Yosemite and Monument Valley. And of
> course this site is always just around the bend, whether one
> is camping early in the day, or running late.

Prime campsites abound along most of the country's waterways, and the search for The Perfect Campsite is one of canoeing's
most enticing challenges. A few guidelines may prove helpful in that
eternal search. After all, it's just around the bend.

WHEN TO CAMP

Some canoeists spend full days on the water, from sunup to
sunset, while others are content to paddle only a few hours each day.
A schedule of some sort is usually maintained just to make sure the
daily miles are evenly distributed. With that in mind, you know
approximately how long you need to be on the water that day.
Rather than rely on chance to find a good site, do some pretrip
research to help you decide when and where to stop. If the river is
well known, there may even be established camps listed and
described in the guidebooks.

In any event, start looking for a campsite early. You're often
competing with other campers, and early arrivals are likely to secure
the best sites. Look for a site well before sunset. Otherwise, darkness
may force you to camp in a rocky spot with no level areas. The night
will be a very long one.

If the campsite you had in mind is occupied and others are
available, good manners say you should move on. In areas where
camping pressure is heavy and the possibilities are few and far
between, you should ask the present occupants for "permisson" to
share the spot. Pressing on might even put your group at risk.
Invariably, though, your neighbors will be people like you, and you
might even make a few friends in the process.

WHERE TO CAMP

On some public lands, you may not have a choice of where to camp if the managing government agency assigns campsites. But in most wilderness areas, the choice of a campsite is up to you. If you're near private land, you should of course take into consideration the rights of landowners. That having been said, most canoe campers believe a suitable campsite should have at least:

- A good landing spot
- A large flat area for tents
- Shade in hot weather
- Shelter in stormy weather
- A pile of driftwood for fires
- A fresh supply of water

These are just the basic principles of campsite selection; a host of other considerations come into play:

MOSQUITOES.

This is an important factor. In areas where mosquitoes and other insects are a problem, beaches and gravel bars are preferable to heavily infested grassy and overgrown areas. A swampy area may usher in a horde of mosquitoes at twilight, and a soft, grassy spot may be full of chiggers.

NATURAL PROTECTION.

In bad weather or windy conditions, you'll want to find a more protected area surrounded by bushes or trees. Caves and rock overhangs may also be helpful in protecting you from the elements.

SHADE.

In hot weather, shade is an obvious attraction. In the desert, its availability is often limited, so keep a close eye out for it.

BREEZE.

If it's hot, a pleasant breeze may be welcome, so look for a more exposed area.

FLOOD CONSIDERATIONS.

Remember, beaches and gravel bars were formed by the river in high water. If it's raining, or if you're located in an area prone to flash flooding, be sure that you have an escape route to higher ground. If a low area exists between you and the shore, a flooding river may create a new channel there, blocking your access to higher terrain.

SANDY BEACHES.

Sandy beaches are clean and feel wonderful underfoot, but there is a downside: Eventually the sand finds its way into *everything*.

DRINKING WATER.

It's nice to have fresh, drinkable water at your campsite, but don't count on it. Instead, fill your water containers at every opportunity (be sure to boil or purify all drinking water).

OFF-THE-WATER ACTIVITIES.

Keep an eye out for places to hike, or perhaps an interesting landmark to investigate.

OTHER ATTRACTIONS.

If you have a choice of sites, you also may want to consider which has a swimming hole, sunshine in the morning, good fishing, and so forth.

ENVIRONMENTAL CONSIDERATIONS.

Beach and gravel bar campsites are preferred because environmental damage can be kept to a minimum. Rivers eventually wash away all evidence of your visit, even footprints. Grassy areas, if heavily used, become trampled and gradually lose their vegetation as boaters pass through. If it's necessary to sleep in a grassy or vegetated area, try to do the cooking on rocks or sand along the shore.

EQUIPMENT ADVANCES.

Gravel bars at first seem inhospitable places for erecting a tent and sleeping bag. But it's well worth the inconvenience if you can get away from bugs and gain an open view. The biggest problem is finding a comfortable place to sleep, and that concern is alleviated by the thick foam or inflatable pads now available. Self-supporting tents also make it easier to pitch a camp in almost any location.

SECURING BOATS

To secure canoes for the night, pull them up on shore, jam the paddles inside, and place rocks on any gear that a strong wind would blow away. To make the boats secure against rising waters, tie them to a tree or large boulder as an extra precaution.

When tying up boats, one thing to watch out for is abrasion. In waves, a canoe can vibrate back and forth against a rock, and that can eventually wear a hole through the material. If your boat is parked in an area where waves are affecting it, pull it far enough up on shore to stop the movement.

THE ROUTINE

While some of the group set up tents, others can get the stove or fire going and the cooking under way. When planning a trip you'll need to decide whether to use a stove or build fires. In some areas where there's little driftwood and the banks have been scoured for wood, stoves are a must. Where driftwood is plentiful, a fire may be acceptable if certain precautions, such as a firepan, are taken. To ensure an evening's supply, pick up driftwood before reaching camp.

A number of other housekeeping chores also need to be taken care of, such as unpacking the kitchen and setting up the latrine. All these activities have environmental consequences, which are covered in detail in the next chapter.

Traceless Camping

CANOEISTS TEND TO BE PROTECTIVE of the path they paddle, which is fortunate for those of us who follow. It may be that canoeists are *more* likely to appreciate the natural world they're escaping to—or *less* likely to spoil the beauty it took so much effort to reach. Whatever the reason, it's important to tread lightly on a resource that can be loved, literally, to death.

GARBAGE

In the total scheme of things, what difference does *one* candy bar wrapper thrown to the wind make? The answer is *a lot,* especially when the single effect is multiplied, as, invariably, it is.

A report compiled by the U.S. Park Service listing the bad habits of river runners in the Grand Canyon proves how destructive we can be:

- Live, standing trees are used for firewood.

- Ash and charcoal from campfires are spread into the ground at rates that far outpace nature's ability to clean the soil.

- Campsites are drastically overused. Fewer than one hundred campsites receive more than 75 percent of all use. At some sites, thirty or forty people camp every night during the busiest four months of the year.

- Over 20 tons of human waste are produced annually by those traveling through the canyon. (Under previous park policy, some five thousand human-waste sites were dug along the river; now wastes must be carried out.)

- "Human debris (food particles, plastic, pop-tops, etc.)," the report states, "exceeds the purging capacities of natural processes. This causes beaches to look and smell like sandboxes found in heavily used public parks."

The rule for disposal of garbage is simple—carry it *all* out. The best equipment for doing so is a plastic bucket with an airtight lid or a plastic garbage bag placed inside a more resilient nylon bag. Keep a small bag handy for use during the day, and be careful to collect even the smallest piece of paper.

If you're using a campfire or charcoal briquettes, burn all trash possible, but remember that aluminum foil packets won't burn and that certain foods (such as eggshells) require more time than a short morning fire. If the garbage can't be burned, dispose of it by placing everything except liquids in the garbage bag. (Grease, in particular, should always be carried out.)

Liquid garbage, such as coffee, soup, and dishwater (containing *biodegradable* soap), should be strained first. The solids remaining can then be thrown into the garbage bag. In wooded areas (which foster rapid decomposition), the liquid can be poured into a single hole dug for that purpose (but at least 100 feet from any area normally used for camping). In wooded areas that are heavily used, it may be better to pour the liquids into the main current of the river, where they will quickly disperse—but first check with the government agency managing the river. In desert regions (which don't foster rapid decomposition), the liquid should *always* be poured into the main current of the river.

One way to avoid garbage in the first place is to plan ahead: Select foods and packaging that will result in as little trash as possible.

THE CAMPFIRE

Staring into the flames of a campfire is for many canoeists the ideal way to end a day of paddling in the wilds. But in some areas, fires have left scars that will take decades or more to heal, and trees have been stripped of their branches (and even cut down) to provide firewood. Even collecting deadwood can damage the environment if not enough is left to replenish the soil with nutrients and to provide shelter for birds and animals.

One alternative to the problem is to ban campfires and to use only stoves for cooking. Doing so would certainly eliminate the need to light fires, but it would also take some of the pleasure out of wilderness travel. Most ecology experts agree that a complete ban on campfires isn't necessary. It's important, however, to treat fires as a luxury and to ensure they have the least possible impact.

Fires may have to be banned, for example, when dry conditions render the fire risk high. In national parks, fire permits may be required and you may have to carry a stove. Such regulations seem restrictive, but they prevent further degradation. Fires, officially permitted or not, are inappropriate in some areas anyway. In particular, fires shouldn't be lit near and above the timberline because of the slow growth rate of trees and the soil's need to be replenished by nutrients from deadwood.

In other areas, fires can be lit even on pristine sites without significant harm to the environment, as long as you take certain precautions. You should leave no sign of your fire, and if possible use a firepan (discussed in detail below). Do *not* leave behind partially burned wood. If you don't use a firepan, and have dug a shallow pit for the fire, be sure that before you move on you refill the pit with the same sod or dirt that you dug from it; spreading dirt and loose vegetation over the site will help conceal it. The ideal place for fires

Campfire at flood level so the river will wash the evidence away.

is below the flood level along rivers, since any traces will eventually be washed away.

Do *not* build a ring of rocks around a fire—the campsite soon becomes littered with blackened rocks. Although the idea is to contain a fire, the best way to do so is to clear the area of flammable materials; a couple of feet is large enough. You should also make sure there are no low branches or tree roots above or below the fire.

Pitch your tent and other gear well away, preferably upwind, so sparks can't cause harm.

If you camp at a well-used site with many rock-ringed fire-places, use an existing one rather than make a new one. Take time to dismantle the other fire rings, removing any ashes and charcoal as garbage. Some designated backcountry sites provide metal fire-boxes, and when present, they should be used.

If you collect wood, do so with care. First and foremost, do not remove wood—even deadwood—from living trees; this is needed by wildlife and adds to the site's attractiveness. Nothing is worse than a campsite surrounded by trees stripped of their lower branches and a ground bare of any fallen wood. In high-use areas, search for wood farther afield. Collect only what you need and use small sticks that can be broken by hand—these are easily burned to ash.

FIREPANS

If you build fires, seriously consider bringing a firepan—a metal container with 3- or 4-inch sides to contain fire and ashes. They're often required by the government agency managing the area, and they're the best way to contain ashes and prevent fire scars. If the firepan doesn't have legs, set it on rocks so it doesn't scorch the ground.

On large-volume or silty rivers, the ashes can be disposed of by dumping them into the river. If you deposit them in an eddy by camp, the ashes eventually wash back to shore, soiling the beaches. Some campsites have become so littered that the soil has turned black. To prevent this, boaters should dump ashes only where the current is strong enough to quickly disperse all traces.

Better yet, you can store the ashes as garbage and carry them out. To prepare ashes for storage, moisten them until they're cool and then shovel them into a container (an old surplus ammo can is ideal). At the next camp, dump the ashes out of the container and into the firepan before starting the fire. As the ashes are burned again at each camp, they're gradually reduced to a fine dust.

If possible, locate the firepan near the river, so high water can clean away any small coals that are accidentally dropped. Use a firepan with at least 3-inch, and preferably 4-inch, sides. An additional safety tip for removing firepans: Throw a little water on the ground as soon as the pan is removed, because the ground below can burn bare feet.

Fires without Pans

If you must build a fire without a firepan, build it where it will have less impact: either below the high-water mark on a rocky shoreline or in a bare spot where it's easy to remove all remains.

Build as small a fire as you can. An entire meal can be cooked with an amazingly small amount of wood. When you're finished with the fire, thoroughly douse it with water and restore the site to its former condition. Throw any blackened rocks into the river.

DISHWASHING

If you're cooking with a camp stove and a single pot, washing dishes is a simple proposition. On luxurious trips with numerous pots, plates, cups, and silverware, the best procedure is a three-bucket wash. In the first bucket add very hot water with *biodegradable* dishwashing soap. Use the second bucket for rinsing, and the third bucket, with a capful of Clorox in it, for disinfecting dishes. It seems involved, but it actually works quickly and prevents intestinal problems that can result from contaminated dishes.

Never dispose of dishwater, leftover food, or soap in side streams or the main river unless you're in the desert or unless you're advised to do so by the government agency managing the river. On a few rivers, such as the Colorado, environmental impact is lessened if the dishwater is first strained of any solid food particles or coffee grounds (which are packed out as garbage), and then disposed of in the main current (not the eddies), rather than on land. *Use this procedure, however, only on rivers where it is specifically recommended.*

On other rivers, the best disposal method is to dig a small hole, carefully removing any sod. Use this same hole for all dishwater while at the campsite (the soil elements will rapidly cause its decomposition). The hole should be situated away from the camp and above the high-water mark. When you're ready to leave, fill in the hole, pack down the soil, and replace the sod so it's indistinguishable from that of its surroundings.

HUMAN-WASTE DISPOSAL

Solid human waste presents both an environmental impact and a hazard to human health. As a result, many government agencies now require that human waste be carried out. It's inevitable that a carry-out disposal system will be implemented on most government lands, and it's a good idea in all heavily traveled areas. The cheapest, most convenient, and most effective means of containing and transporting this waste is an airtight toilet box sold by various boating supply companies. The necessary items include:

- Metal river toilet box of approximately 18″ x 14″ x 8″ size (surplus ammunition boxes work well if they're airtight)
- Toilet seat
- Chemical deodorant (such as dry lime, AquaChem, or chlorine bleach)
- Toilet paper, water dispenser, and hand soap

The system is easy to set up. Pour a small amount of the dry lime or chemical deodorant into the toilet box and place the toilet seat on top (the water dispenser and hand soap can be situated nearby). Plastic bags should not be used with this system because they aren't biodegradable.

Chemical deodorants are important because they reduce bacterial growth and the production of methane gas. The amount of chemical deodorant needed depends on the type used: A few ounces a day of liquid deodorant is sufficient for six or seven people, while approximately twice as much chlorine bleach is required. The number of toilet boxes needed depends on the number of people and the length of the trip; on average, it's possible to containerize a weeklong trip for ten people in one box. After the trip, the waste should be deposited in an approved solid waste landfill.

Side hikes also require sanitary waste disposal, but of a slightly different kind. To reduce impact, bury the waste (after carefully burning the toilet paper) in a hole about 6 inches deep, the best depth for soil elements that cause rapid decomposition. Carry a small backpacker's trowel, and make the hole at least 100 feet from the river's high-water line and away from any area normally used for camping.

5

The Kitchen

AMONG CANOEISTS, cooking styles vary. Some boaters prefer lavish, four-course meals with fresh fruits and vegetables, while others prefer the lean and easy-to-prepare backpacker fare of dehydrated and freeze-dried foods. How you eat will largely determine the type and amount of cooking gear you'll need. With either extreme, modern technology has made the job easier.

GENERAL CONSIDERATIONS

Cookware typically consists of the standard set of aluminum or stainless-steel nesting pots, which are lightweight and compact. A cast-iron or Teflon-coated griddle and frying pan may come in handy for certain menus. A lot of canoeists use the old-fashioned Dutch oven, which is extremely versatile (see the discussion later in this chapter). Although not as widely used, the folding aluminum reflector oven, first devised by French-Canadian voyageurs, is considered by many canoeing gourmands to be unequaled for baking.

Speaking of heat control, some boaters still favor cooking over an open fire, which is usually acceptable as long as a firepan is used to contain the ashes and charcoal produced. Other river cooks, however, prefer the consistent heat of a white-gas or propane stove. The number of models has proliferated, and their sophistication and durability have gone a long way in making the cook's life an easier one.

Depending on the menu, you'll need to consider your requirements for other cooking utensils, such as a can opener, serving fork, cooking spoon, serving spoon, carving knife, paring knife, potato peeler, turning spatula, tongs, and so on. A roll-up pouch with compartments allows for better organization of these utensils. Refillable polyethylene tubes, with removable clips on the end, are also handy for storing butter and other spreadables. Also useful are a hard-plastic egg carton and a spice container with slots for half a dozen spices. Now there's even a miniature espresso maker for camp stoves.

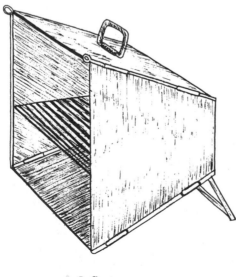

Reflector oven

A necessity, of course, is a pair of pot-gripper pliers for handling hot cookware.

If you've ever had a pot of dinner fall off a rock and into the sand, you'll appreciate the steady surface of a table designed just for campers. The plastic-covered, wooden-slatted version, which rolls up like a sleeping pad, is especially compact and quite sturdy.

CAMP STOVES

Camp stoves offer a number of advantages: They reduce the need for campfires (and their resulting environmental impact), and they ensure that you have hot food and drink when you want them.

At the end of a long day, when you're pitching camp and feeling tired, setting up a stove is easy. Gathering wood and building a fire takes more time and effort. In foul weather, a stove enables you to cook hot meals in the warmth and shelter of your tent.

Among the choice of stoves, the differences in makes and models are significant. In some situations a malfunctioning stove is a nuisance. At other times it poses a serious problem, particularly if you're relying on it and lighting a campfire is impossible. Some

Stoves are easy on the environment and chef alike.

stoves work well in the cold and wind, while others don't. Waiting for a stove to produce hot water when you're wet and cold is annoying, but if you're on the verge of hypothermia, it's life-threatening.

Charts comparing the weights, fuel consumption, and boiling times of various stoves can be misleading. Many factors affecting a stove's performance in the field can't be duplicated in a controlled environment, and individual stoves of the same model can also perform differently.

A stove needs to fulfill a number of criteria. It must be capable of bringing water to a boil under the worst conditions you're likely to encounter, it must be small and light enough to pack, and it must be simple to operate. Stability is important too, particularly when the stove is used with large pans.

FUELS

The availability of fuel in the areas you plan to visit may determine the stove you select. The choice is between liquid fuel (in the form of alcohol, kerosene, or white gas) and cartridges (containing butane or butane/propane).

Fuel consumption depends upon the type of stove you have, the weather, and the type of cooking you do. If you cook three meals a day and use foods with long cooking times, you'll obviously use more fuel than someone who only boils water for a freeze-dried dinner at night.

WHITE GAS.

White gas is the most efficient stove fuel—it lights easily and burns very hot. Automobile fuel can sometimes be used, but it quickly clogs fuel jets (many stove makers state firmly that it shouldn't be used). White-gas stoves should be run on specially refined fuel such as Coleman Fuel. Although white gas is volatile, ignites easily if spilled, and requires a lot of care, in North America it's generally the only fuel you can find just about anywhere.

White-gas stoves burn the fuel as it's vaporized, which means that it has to be pressurized. In the simplest models, the fuel is transmitted from the tank to the burner via a wick that leads into the fuel line. These stoves have to be preheated or primed before they're lit, so that the fuel can vaporize before passing through the jet. Those models with pressure pumps make the stove easier to light.

Because they burn pressurized fuel, these stoves can flare badly during lighting, so they must be used with care if they're inside a tent. They operate best when half to three-quarters full, and they should never be completely filled since the fuel needs to expand to pressurize the stove fully.

White-gas stoves have one of two types of burners: roarer or ported. The roarer uses a stream of vaporized fuel that's pushed out of the jet, ignites, and hits a burner plate, which spreads it out into a ring of flame. Not surprisingly, roarer-type burners are noisy. In ported burners, the flames come out of a ring of jets, just as in a kitchen gas range. Ported burners are much quieter. Neither type seems more efficient than the other, though ported ones are easier to control and thus better for simmering.

BUTANE AND PROPANE.

Light, clean, simple to use, cartridge stoves are the choice of many canoeists. The fuel is liquid petroleum gas, kept under pressure in a sealed cartridge. The most popular version is pure butane, which is relatively cheap, though sometimes difficult to find. Because of the cartridge's low pressure (necessary because the cartridge walls are thin to keep the weight down), the butane won't vaporize in temperatures much below 40 degrees.

As the cartridge empties and the pressure drops, the burning rate of the stove falls until it won't bring water to a boil. Cartridges with a mixture of butane and propane work better in below-freezing temperatures because propane vaporizes at a much lower temperature than butane. Propane, however, is so volatile that it requires heavy, thick-walled containers. Lightweight cartridges are usually 85 percent butane and 15 percent propane.

All cartridge stoves have quiet, ported burners. The heat output is easily adjusted, making them excellent for simmering, but the flame must be protected from the wind. Most come with small windscreens, but you may need a separate windscreen for windy conditions. There are two types of cartridges: those with a self-sealing valve that allows them to be removed from the stove at any time, and those that must be left in place until they're empty.

KEROSENE.

Kerosene is the traditional stove fuel. It's easily obtained, reasonably cheap, and burns hot. Kerosene won't ignite easily, so it's safer than white gas if spilled. Conversely, it's more difficult to light, usually requiring a separate priming fuel such as solid-fuel tablets or paste. Kerosene tends to flare during lighting, so it should always be ignited outside a tent. It's a messy fuel, it stains badly, it leaves a strong odor, and it takes a long time to evaporate. But many canoeists swear by it.

Kerosene stoves have noisy roarer burners and are relatively heavy. The flame is controlled by opening a valve and releasing some of the pressure. Although the flame is powerful and most models have small windscreens to protect the burners, the efficiency of these stoves can be increased with the use of a full windscreen in breezy conditions.

ALCOHOL.

Fuel for alcohol stoves is available as denatured alcohol or marine stove fuel. It can be hard to find (look for it in hardware stores and backpacking shops) as well as expensive. It's the only fuel not derived from petroleum and the only one burned nonpressurized as a liquid, which makes it safer. It's clean, too, evaporating quickly if spilled. For these reasons, it's a good fuel anytime you'll be cooking regularly in the tent. But it's not a hot fuel, producing only half as much heat as the same weight of gasoline or kerosene.

Alcohol stoves can be set up quickly and have little that can go wrong; the only maintenance needed is to prick the jets occasionally. These stoves are silent and safe, but you need to be careful when using them in daylight because the flame is invisible. Because a full burner only lasts half an hour, refilling the stove is often necessary, and inadvertently filling a still-burning stove must be carefully avoided.

Safety and Maintenance

All stoves are potentially dangerous and should be used cautiously. Before you light a stove, always check that attachments to fuel tanks or cartridges are secure, tank caps and fuel-bottle tops tight, and controls turned off. Carefully study and practice the instructions that come with it.

Stoves are most dangerous during lighting, when they can flare badly. For this reason, never hold your head over a stove when you light it. Do *not* light a stove that's close to any flammable material, particularly your tent. Light it in open air whenever possible, even if this means placing it in the rain and bringing it inside the tent when it's burning.

A stove should also be refilled with care, after you've made sure there are no burning candles, other lit stoves, or campfires nearby. This applies whether you're changing a butane cartridge or pouring fuel into a white-gas stove tank. Refuel outside your tent to prevent spillage damage.

Overheating of cartridges or fuel tanks is another potential hazard. Make sure enough air flows around the tank or cartridge and that the windscreen doesn't completely surround the stove. To avoid overheating, don't use rocks to stabilize stoves, and if you have large pans that overhang the burner, periodically check to see if too much heat is being reflected off the pans onto the tank.

Another real threat of a stove inside a tent is carbon monoxide poisoning, which can be fatal. All stoves consume oxygen and give off this odorless, colorless gas, so ventilation is required.

Most stoves need little maintenance. Except for those with built-in self-cleaning needles, the jets of a stove may need cleaning with the thin wire stove-prickers that come with most models. Rubber seals on tank caps and cartridge attachment points should be checked periodically, lubricated if necessary, and replaced if worn.

Fuel Containers

There are many plastic and metal fuel bottles available. Plastic ones are fine for alcohol, but metal bottles are better for volatile fuels such as gasoline or kerosene. Fuel bottles must be sturdy, and they need a well-sealed, leakproof cap. Almost standard are the cylindrical Swiss-made Sigg bottles, which are extremely tough.

It's almost impossible to fill small fuel tanks directly from fuel bottles without spillage. But, fortunately, a number of ingenious devices have been developed to prevent this. One has a small plastic spout inserted in one side and a tiny hole drilled in the other. By placing a finger over the hole, you can control the flow.

Accessories

All stoves need a windscreen to function efficiently. Whatever windscreen you use, it should extend well above the burner to be effective.

To simplify the lighting of white-gas stoves, especially in cold weather, there's a small pump you can purchase to replace the fuel cap. But pumps must be used carefully to avoid overpressurizing the tank. Kerosene stoves need to be primed, and there are various flammable pastes for the purpose.

A recent innovation is the heat exchanger, which is a corrugated aluminum collar that fits around the stove and reduces boiling time by directing more heat up the sides of the pan.

FIRE STARTERS

Matches are essential for lighting fires and starting stoves, and it's a good idea to carry several boxes of strike-anywhere ones, each box sealed in a small plastic bag. Waterproof match containers are also available.

It's unlikely that several boxes kept in different places will become soaked, but it can happen, so carrying an emergency fire starter of some kind is a good idea. A box of waterproof and windproof matches is ideal.

An alternative to matches is a cigarette lighter. Just the spark from a lighter will ignite white-gas and butane stoves (though not kerosene or alcohol), and if the lighter gets wet, it's easily dried, while a sodden box of matches is useless.

More esoteric fire lighters are also available. Flint and magnesium ones work off chippings scraped from a magnesium block, and the chippings are ignited by sparks caused by drawing a knife across a flint. Another model has a brass "match" that lights a gasoline-soaked wick when struck. Carrying one of these models is recommended on remote trips.

UTENSILS

Your cooking habits will no doubt determine the amount of kitchen gear you bring. One advantage of minimal cooking is that it requires minimal tools.

PANS.

Many stoves come with pans and windscreens designed specifically for that stove. Tight-fitting lids are important because they help water boil faster. Many lids are designed to double as frying pans, but most don't work very well and a separate nonstick frying pan is better.

POT GRABS.

Far superior to fixed pot handles are simple two-piece pot grabs that clamp onto the edge of the pan when the handles are pressed together. Not all are of good quality; some of the thin aluminum ones soon distort and twist out of shape. To make tight-fitting lids easy to lift off pans, put the lids on upside down with the rims pointing upward.

MUGS.

Plastic mugs are light and cheap but not very durable; they soon develop uncleanable scratches and cracks. They also retain tastes, which relegates them to one type of liquid. Mugs made of Lexan plastic are better: They don't retain tastes and are unbreakable.

The alternative to plastic is stainless steel (aluminum retains heat, so it's less practical). Stainless steel, however, is ideal: It remains cool, doesn't taint, doesn't scratch, and is long-lasting. The classic is the Sierra Club cup with its shallow profile and wire handle.

EATING UTENSILS.

Lexan plastic also works for cutlery, but it does discolor and can be broken. Metal cutlery lasts much longer.

BEAR PROOFING

In some areas, bears (and other animals) can be a threat to your food supply, so it takes a little ingenuity to foil their efforts. If you're camped near trees, hang your food bag from a low branch to protect it from animals. In areas where bears raid campsites, food bags need to be hung at least 12 feet above the ground and 10 feet away from the trunk of the tree. They should also be 6 feet below any branch.

There are various ways to meet these demands, all requiring 50 feet or more of nylon line. The simplest method is to tie a rock to the end of the line, throw it over a branch about 20 feet above the ground and 10 feet from the trunk, haul up the food until the bottom of the bag is 12 feet or more high, then tie off the line around the trunk of the tree.

With smaller trees, you may have to suspend food bags between two trees about 25 feet apart, which involves throwing one end of the weighted line over a branch, tying it off, and then repeating the process with the other end over a branch of the second tree. Keep the line between the

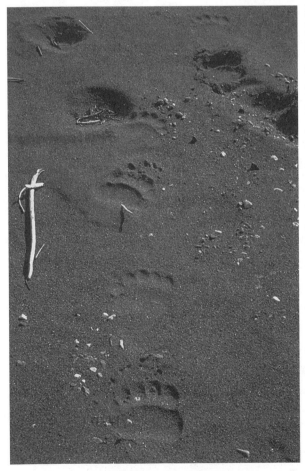

Fresh Alaskan bear prints.

two trees within reach so you can tie the food bag to it. Then haul the bag up until it's halfway between the trees and about 12 feet off the ground.

In a few areas, bears have learned that breaking a line rewards them with a bag of food. In these places, neither of these methods works. Instead, you must use a counterbalance system, which involves throwing the line over a branch that's at least 25 feet high, tying a food bag to the end of the line, and hauling it up to the branch. You then tie a second food bag (or bag of rocks if you haven't enough food) to the other end of the line. Then heave the second bag into the air (or use a stick to pull down the other bag) so that both bags end up 12 feet or more above the ground and 10 feet from the tree trunk. If you leave a loop of line at the top of one of the bags, you can hook it with a stick to pull the bags down the next morning.

If you camp far from trees, store food at least 100 yards away from your tent in airtight plastic bags. You might also consider "bear-proof" surplus ammunition boxes, though they're bulky.

Bears are attracted to food by smell, so they may consider items such as toothpaste, soap, insect repellent, sunscreen, food-stained clothing, dishrags, and dirty pots and pans to be food. Hang them with your food and keep them out of your tent.

WATER PURIFICATION

A canoe trip by definition involves water, but the problem is deciding whether it's safe to drink. Water clarity is, unfortunately, not an indication of purity. Even the most sparkling, crystal-clear mountain stream may be unsafe to drink because of invisible contaminants, including a wide variety of microorganisms that cause diarrhea and dysentery—sometimes mild, sometimes severe.

Giardiasis, caused by the protozoan *Giardia lamblia,* which lives in the intestines of humans and animals, is a virulent stomach disorder curable only by antibiotics. It's transferred through water in the form of cysts and feces (another reason always to situate toilets well away from water). The symptoms of giardiasis appear a few weeks after the protozoan is ingested, and they include diarrhea, stomachache, bloating, and nausea. Because these symptoms occur in other stomach disorders as well, only a stool analysis can confirm infection.

If you're one of the unlucky people to become infected with giardiasis, there are a couple of prescription antibiotics that can cure the disease. However, prevention is the preferable measure.

Water can be purified by boiling it, treating it with chemicals, and filtering it. Boiling is the surest way to kill dangerous organisms, but it's impractical—except perhaps for water used in camp—because boiling uses fuel and takes time. Iodine and chlorine tablets are lightweight and simple to use; but neither is fully effective, though iodine is better than chlorine. Both make the water taste unpleasant, so you'll want to add fruit-flavored mixes to make it drinkable.

Potable Aqua is a common brand of iodine tablets, which have a limited shelf life, so you should buy a fresh supply at least annually. Iodine crystals are reputedly more effective than tablets; kits containing iodine crystals, thermometer, and instructions can be

Taking time out to purify drinking water.

The passage from one life to another

Canoeing the jagged plateau known as the Ozarks

Feast on the flood

NATURAL DISTRACTIONS
AT EVERY BEND

DUSK ON UTAH'S GREEN RIVER

DESERT IN BLOOM

THE WINDSWEPT
RIDGES AND CRAGS
OF THE RIO GRANDE

CONTEMPLATING CANADA'S NAHANNI RIVER

OFF-RIVER
DIVERSIONS BECKON

CAMPSITE ON ALASKA'S TATSHENSHINI RIVER

THE QUIETUDE OF NATURE

THE WAY OF
THE WILDERNESS

THE SOLITUDE OF AN AFTERNOON HIKE

THE REST OF THE WORLD SEEMS FAR AWAY

purchased at most outdoor stores. Use iodine carefully; too much will poison you.

Filtration is probably the best treatment. There are a number of lightweight, handheld models available; many have replaceable charcoal-based filters that screen out pesticides and chemicals (which boiling won't do), as well as microorganisms larger than 0.4 micron. The most expensive of these filters is the Swiss-made Katadyn Pocket Water Filter, whose silver-quartz-impregnated ceramic filter screens out organisms larger than 0.2 micron.

Water Bottles

Water containers are available in a wide variety of shapes, sizes, and materials. Aluminum keeps liquids cool in summer, but unless it's lacquered inside, it contaminates water containing drink mixes. The heavy-duty Nalgene-brand plastic bottles have wide mouths for easy filling and caps that don't leak. Special insulated covers are available.

For camp use, you'll need a larger water container. A lot of canoeists take along the ubiquitous 5-gallon water containers made of collapsible plastic, but they spring holes quickly. More sturdy are water bags with a plastic inner bladder and a tough nylon outer bag.

In really cold weather, a thermos-type flask can be useful (the best ones are unbreakable stainless steel). If you fill it before leaving camp, you can enjoy hot drinks during the day. This eliminates the need to stop and fire up the stove.

6

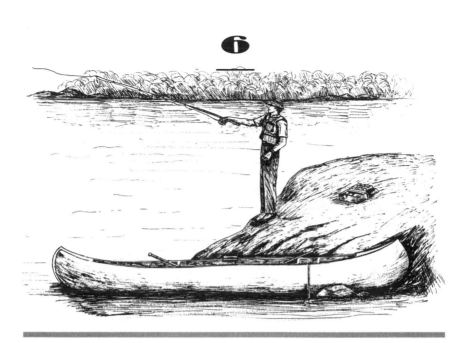

Wilderness Cuisine

IN SOME CANOEING CIRCLES, boaters are as well known for the hash they sling as for the paddles they swing. As a result, culinary skills can become an important part of the canoeing experience. Bert Loper, an early pre–World War II river runner of the West, once wrote in his diary: "Have a big pot of beans on cooking. I have developed the most abnormal appetite that a mortal ever possessed. I start out in the morning with a bucket of cold beans, bacon, and bread, and eat the entire thing during the day." Most of us can relate to Bert's appetite, but we usually expect to eat a little better than he did.

NUTRITION

How scientific do you have to be when selecting foods for a wilderness canoe trip? Not very, as long as you use good sense and plan reasonably well-balanced meals. What works at home will work in the wilds, with one exception: calories! You'll need lots of them—4,000 a day if you're really paddling hard.

Fortunately, you don't need to be too exacting in determining "nutritional value," but it's important to balance your daily intake of foods so they correspond roughly to the following:

CARBOHYDRATES.

Carbohydrates provide quick energy and should supply at least 50 percent of your daily caloric requirement. Foods that contain carbohydrates include breads, cereals, honey, jam, dehydrated fruits, and, of course, candy.

FATS.

Fats contain about twice as many calories per pound as carbohydrates and are the body's major source of stored energy. Generally speaking, fats should provide about 20 to 25 percent of your calories, and for a rigorous trip, even more. Foods containing fats are margarine, cooking oil, nuts, peanut butter, cheese, bacon, and sausage.

PROTEINS.

Wilderness canoeing is a strenuous activity, so you'll need more protein than normal: a hearty breakfast of oat or wheat cereal with milk; a lunch that includes cheese, beef jerky, peanut butter, or sausage (which are sources of protein as well as fat); and a supper that contains meat or beans.

WEIGHT AND BULK

Weight and bulk don't matter much on one- or two-night jaunts, but they can be a concern on longer trips. Fresh and canned foods are bulky and heavy, so dried foods are the best choice. The simplest method of drying food is under a hot sun. Because this doesn't remove as much moisture as other methods, it's not used for many foods (though some fruits are sun-dried). Air-drying, a process in which the food is spun in a drum or arranged on trays through which hot air is blown, produces dehydrated foods. But reconstituted dehydrated foods have a reputation for poor taste.

The most expensive means of extracting water from food is the freeze-drying process, in which food is frozen so quickly that its moisture turns to ice. The food is then placed in a low-temperature vacuum, where the ice turns directly into vapor without passing through a liquid state. Freeze-dried food is costly, but it does taste better. Because the food can be cooked before being freeze-dried, you only need to add boiling water.

To supplement your dried foods, you'll need lots of calories on a rigorous outing, and that means extra bread, peanut butter, margarine, nuts, cereals, and cheese. The food you take should be light-weight, slow to spoil, easy to prepare, and stable in hot weather.

PACKING SUGGESTIONS

Organizing your meals before you hit the water will repay itself many times over. To eliminate confusion and shorten preparation times, package each meal as a complete unit. Remove all unnecessary cardboard and paper wrappers to save weight, space, and the amount of trash you'll have to pack out. Label the bags as "B-1" (breakfast on the first day), "L-2" (lunch on the second day), and so forth.

Sugar, flour, drink mixes, and other "pourable solids" are best premeasured and placed in sturdy plastic Ziploc bags. Breakable and crushable items, such as crackers, cheese, and candy bars, should be packed inside rigid cardboard containers (which can be burned as the foods stored inside are consumed). Liquids are best carried in plastic bottles with screw-cap lids; Nalgene-brand containers (available at most camping stores) seem to be the most reliable.

COOKING TIMES

The time food takes to cook affects the amount of fuel you need to carry and the amount of time you'll have to wait. When you're exhausted and hungry and a storm is raging all around, knowing your dinner will be ready in five minutes rather than thirty can be important. As you gain altitude, water takes longer to boil; at 5,000 feet, the cooking time is twice that at sea level.

Many foods, from cup-of-soups to eat-from-the-packet, freeze-dried meals, don't require any cooking, just boiling water and a quick stir. But then, they don't usually taste as good as meals that require a little simmering. Most meals need five to ten minutes, a good compromise between speed and taste.

Cooking times for some dried foods can be reduced by pre-soaking. This works with vegetables, meat, and legumes, but not pasta or rice. Some canoeists soak food in a capped bottle during the day so it's ready for cooking at night.

REFRIGERATION

One beauty of a canoe is its ability to accommodate an ice chest. On an overnight trip, keeping fresh foods from spoiling isn't a problem. Larger parties, with a number of ice chests, can keep food cold for longer periods of time by reducing the opening of each ice chest, which causes ice to melt faster. Some canoeists find that by using dry ice and sealing the ice chests not in use with duct tape they can keep ice for a week or more. In any event, using fresh foods early in the trip and relying on dried foods later on provides a nice variety in the menu.

SUGGESTED MENUS

Food suitable for canoeing can be found in supermarkets, health food stores, and outdoor shops. Prices are lowest in supermarkets, which usually have all the foods you need, with perhaps the exception of freeze-dried meals. Check cooking times carefully; one packet of soup may take five minutes to cook while an almost identical one takes twenty-five. Health food stores have a wider variety of cereals, dried fruits, and grain bars than supermarkets, though the number of supermarkets selling these foods is increasing. You'll find foods specifically made for backpackers and mountaineers in outdoor stores; these are lightweight and low in bulk, though expensive.

Lightweight Meals

Meals on canoe trips can be as simple as you wish to make them—a style many canoeists prefer because it allows them to spend more time on the water. Here's a sampling of some lightweight, simple menus:

BREAKFASTS.

Regardless of the weather, a hot drink of tea, instant coffee, or hot chocolate is a nice way of starting the day. The main meal for a lightweight breakfast could be:

- Instant hot cereals (oatmeal, cream of wheat, etc.)
- Cold cereals (granola, Grape Nuts, etc., using powdered milk or the new vacuum-packed milk that doesn't need refrigeration)
- Freeze-dried breakfasts (available at backpacking and outdoor stores)
- Snack foods that don't require cooking (cheese, crackers, salami, jerky, nuts, dried fruit, etc.)

LUNCHES.

In order to save time, lunch typically isn't cooked. Some canoeists schedule a special day in which they cook lunch, but this usually takes too much time to be done every day. It is, however, a good idea to bring some extra hot drinks or soup mixes for cold, rainy days. Some suggestions for a lightweight lunch:

- Bread (for sandwiches)
- Salami
- Canned fish (tuna, salmon, kippers, sardines, etc.)
- Canned meat (sandwich spreads, chicken, beef, etc.)
- Jerky
- Crackers
- Cheese
- Dried fruits (raisins, apples, apricots, pears, etc.)
- Various types of candies (sugar or honey)
- Peanut butter
- Granola
- Nuts (cashews, sunflower, etc.)
- Gorp (mixture of raisins, nuts, chocolate chips, etc.)

SUPPERS.

Soups or hot drinks are a quick predinner warm-up. The main course can consist of freeze-dried dinners, the lightest and most convenient meal there is. The best types of freeze-dried dinners are those to which you add hot water, then wait several minutes before eating. Unfortunately, the convenience of freeze-dried dinners comes with a price. You can put together many fine nutritional, lightweight meals by buying products at your local supermarket, where various dehydrated foods and "convenience" meals are available (such as beef stroganoff, chicken tetrazzini, etc.). For simplicity, most lightweight meals are cooked in one pot, though some canoeists prepare separate dishes.

For Further Reading. Try *The One Pan Gourmet,* by Diane Jacobson.

Luxurious Meals

A lot of canoeists find eating to be an important part of their outdoor experience, so they don't mind spending a little time and effort in the kitchen. The results can be extraordinary.

BREAKFASTS.

A good warm-up for a luxurious breakfast is a hot drink of coffee, tea, or cocoa. Some people like to serve fruit juices along with the main meal. The main course can consist of such typical morning meals as:

- Bacon and eggs
- Pancakes
- Omelets (vegetarian, Spanish, etc.)
- Eggs (scrambled, fried, poached, etc.)
- Fruit
- Hash browns
- Egg and potato casseroles
- Quiches
- French toast

LUNCHES.

Since cooking is time-consuming, most lunches are served cold. Typical items include:

- Bread
- Rolls
- Bagels
- Lunch meats (turkey, beef, corned beef, bologna, etc.)
- Salami or sausage
- Cheese
- Peanut butter

- Jam
- Tuna fish
- Pickles
- Mayonnaise, mustard, catsup
- Fresh fruit
- Candy and cookies

SUPPERS.

Just about everything goes for suppers on luxury-style trips. With Dutch ovens, practically any meal you cook at home can be served in the wilds.

To warm up after a long day on the water, start with a soup. Use packaged mixes or canned soups, or even start from scratch. The primary course can center on a meat dish such as steak, hamburgers, pork chops, or chicken; or it can be vegetarian. Various salads (lettuce, fruit, bean, or potato) balance out the main meal, and bread or biscuits can also be served. For a nightcap, dessert—pies,

As luxurious as you please.

cakes, brownies, or popcorn—is often prepared later in the evening when everyone is gathered around the fire.

For Further Reading. Get a copy of *River Runners Recipes,* by Patricia McCairen.

Snacks

A staple snack food is that mixture of dried fruit, nuts, and seeds known as trail mix or "gorp" (which stands for Good Old Raisins and Peanuts). At its most basic, it consists of peanuts and raisins, but more sophisticated mixes include bits of dried fruit (favorites are papaya, pineapple, and dates), a range of nuts, coconut, chocolate chips, sunflower and sesame seeds, granola, and anything else you like.

Savory snacks such as crispbread or crackers and a cheese or vegetable spread make a pleasant contrast. Spreads that come in easy-to-use squeeze tubes are especially convenient. Or you can transfer spreads into squeeze tubes specially designed for reuse.

Spices

There are various ways to enhance the taste of any meal. Adding herbs and spices, garlic powder, cloves, curry or chili powder, and black pepper helps. Margarine, cheese, and milk powder add calories as well as taste. Packets of soup can provide flavoring or the base for a meal with pasta and rice.

SAMPLE RECIPES

The following are a number of recipes to get you started on your way to culinary canoeing. After a few seasons of camping by canoe, you'll no doubt develop your own repertoire.

Voyageur Chili (serves 2)

1 lb. stew beef or steak, cut into ½" cubes
1 medium onion, chopped
1 garlic clove, minced
2 tablespoons vegetable oil

1 16-ounce can diced tomatoes
2 tablespoons chili powder
1 teaspoon ground cumin
1 teaspoon salt
2 cans pinto beans

☞ In frying pan, cook beef, onion, and garlic in oil until beef is browned and onions tender. Add tomatoes and spices. Bring to boil and reduce heat. Simmer covered for about 30 minutes, or until meat is tender. Add beans and simmer 5 more minutes.

Paddler's Stir-Fry Vegetables (serves 2)

4 teaspoons peanut oil
3 cups mixed vegetables (green beans, pea pods, carrots, diced onions, mushrooms, green or red peppers)
2 tablespoons soy sauce
pepper to taste

☞ Heat frying pan over high flame. Add oil and let heat. Add vegetables and stir-fry for about 2 to 3 minutes. Add soy sauce and pepper. Toss and stir-fry for another minute. Serve over precooked rice.

Hell's Canyon Chicken Cacciatore (serves 2)

1 lb. boned chicken
salt and pepper to taste
garlic powder to taste
olive oil
1 large onion, sliced
1 medium green pepper, sliced
2 6-ounce cans tomato paste
2 cups water
6 to 8 mushrooms, sliced
½ teaspoon oregano

☞ Coat chicken with salt, pepper, and garlic powder. Heat oil in pan; add chicken and brown. Remove chicken and add onion and green pepper to pan and sauté until tender. Add tomato paste, water, mushrooms, oregano, and chicken. Cover and cook for 30 minutes over medium flame.

Moose River Carrot and Lentil Stew (serves 2)

1 cup lentils
2 large carrots, diced
1 large onion, diced
2 garlic cloves, crushed
2 large tomatoes
2 teaspoons parsley
2 bay leaves
pinch of salt
black pepper and chili powder to taste

☞ Add lentils and vegetables to 8 cups cold water, bring to a boil, then simmer 45 minutes or until lentils are soft. Add salt and spices. Cooking time can be shortened if lentils are soaked beforehand in hot water.

Boundary Waters Blueberry Cobbler (serves 2)

1 cup blueberries
1 teaspoon cinnamon
½ teaspoon nutmeg
1 teaspoon flour
2 cups Bisquick
4 tablespoons margarine
½ cup sugar
2 eggs, beaten
1 cup milk

☞ In Dutch oven, combine blueberries, spices, and flour. In bowl, mix all other ingredients and pour over fruit mixture. Bake in Dutch oven for about 30 minutes, or until top layer is brown.

DUTCH OVEN COOKERY

The Dutch oven—that kettlelike cast-iron cooking pot with short legs, rimmed cover, and bail—has proven itself to be an amazingly versatile piece of cookware. Many outdoor chefs claim that no other culinary device can produce such delicious meals with so little skill. The range of cooking is great—baking, stewing, roasting, and frying. Even the most inexperienced cook can turn out tasty stews, casseroles, chili, sourdough bread, and cobblers.

The traditional D.O. is made of cast iron, which renders it a fairly heavy and durable piece of gear. With a high tolerance for the extreme temperatures of a campfire, cast iron diffuses heat over the entire surface of the oven, allowing foods to be cooked evenly without burning. After prolonged use, it develops a unique seasoning.

Dutch oven

Dutch ovens made of cast aluminum have recently been introduced as an alternative to cast iron. Their biggest advantage is their weight—about half that of cast-iron ovens. Aluminum (which doesn't season as cast iron does) is also rustproof and requires less heat. The aluminum D.O.'s, however, have the disadvantage of being more sensitive to heat variations, and therefore more difficult to cook with.

Dutch ovens range from 8 to 16 inches in diameter, but the most popular sizes are the 10- and 12-inch diameters. The 10-inch oven has a capacity of about 4½ quarts, and the 12-inch oven, 7 quarts. Before buying an oven, carefully check out its features. Most important, make sure it has short legs to raise it above the ground, allowing coals to be placed underneath. The legs should be well spaced to keep the oven steady, and the lid must have a raised lip for holding coals on top.

Seasoning and Care

To obtain its unique seasoning, a new cast-iron oven needs to be broken in by the following method. Slowly melt a tablespoon of shortening in the heated D.O., making sure to coat the bottom surface thoroughly. Remove the D.O. from the heat, and with a paper towel thoroughly coat the inside surfaces with shortening. Then, using another paper towel, wipe off the excess shortening. The new D.O. is now ready.

After each use, wash the oven with a mild soap. (Never use strong detergents.) Then place the D.O. on the fire long enough to dry it thoroughly. When it's dry, place a little shortening in the oven and spread it around with a paper towel. This drying and recoating process should be repeated until the D.O. is well seasoned.

Always remember that one of the biggest problems of cast iron is rust. If the D.O. ever gets rusty or loses its seasoning through excessive scrubbing, it's necessary to reseason the oven. (A metallic taste or discolored food indicates that the oven has lost its seasoning, even though this might not be evident from the oven's appearance.) To reseason the oven, scour it with steel wool, wash it with soap and water, and dry it thoroughly. Now coat the inner surfaces of the oven with shortening and place the D.O. in your electric oven at home (on warm setting) for about two hours. Wipe the D.O. thoroughly with a paper towel and it's again ready for use.

Aluminum D.O.'s don't require the seasoning of cast iron, and they have a higher tolerance for ordinary dishwashing methods (allowing the use of detergents and scouring pads). Aluminum ovens, however, may warp (or possibly melt) if exposed to the excessive heat of a large campfire. Regardless of whether the Dutch oven is cast iron or aluminum, a few precautions should be taken. Never pour cold water into a hot oven, and be careful not to drop the D.O., since it might crack, rendering it inefficient (and virtually useless) because of heat loss.

Preparation of Coals

The first step in cooking with the Dutch oven is the preparation of coals. Whether you use wood or briquettes, heating the coals on a grill above the fire will prevent them from being mixed with sand and ashes, which keep air away and prevent the coals from burning hot. It's also a good idea to use a metal firepan to contain the fire (as well as the ashes and charcoal it produces) and to reduce scarring of the ground.

Although charcoal lumps ignite and heat faster than briquettes, they also burn faster, making them suitable for foods with a short cooking time. Briquettes last longer than lumps and provide a more reliable and consistent heat. Natural wood in the form of driftwood or fallen branches will also produce good coals for cooking if caution is taken in the selection of wood; try to use hardwoods that produce hot, long-burning coals with an even heat.

Cooking with the Dutch Oven

Heat distribution is the most important aspect of Dutch oven cooking. When placing coals on top of the oven, arrange them on the edge of the lid and nearly touching each other. For coals underneath, position them close to (but not touching) the bottom and about an inch in from the outside edge.

Experience will tell you how many coals are needed on the top and bottom of the oven, but distribution will depend on the type of cooking you do. For stewing, there should be a roughly equal number of coals on top and bottom, with perhaps slightly more on top. For baking, most of the coals—about three-quarters—should be on top to prevent burning the batter on the bottom. Another helpful guideline: Approximately twenty-five briquettes is equivalent to a 375-degree oven.

Wood coals are more difficult to cook with than briquettes simply because various woods burn at different temperatures. Blowing the ashes off the coals will increase heat, and rotating the lid (but not lifting it) will even out the temperature. Avoid lifting the lid and looking to check on the food. Each time you look, you lose five to ten minutes' cooking time.

Baking with the Dutch Oven

Baking is the specialty of Dutch oven cooking, and the cook with a flair for cobblers has achieved the pinnacle of the art. Fortunately, successful baking is easy if a few basic steps are followed. First, prepare the batter from scratch or with a ready-made mix such as Bisquick. Before pouring in the batter, grease the oven well with shortening or cooking oil.

If you're preparing a cobbler, put the fruit on the bottom and pour the batter on top. Place about three-quarters of the coals on the lid and use the remainder underneath—but not touching—the oven. If the recipe requires preheating, the D.O. should be preheated just like your oven at home.

To check whether the baking is done, quickly lift the lid and stick a fork or twig through the middle of the pastry. If it comes out clean, the cooking is done—and the enjoyment begins.

For Further Reading. Highly recommended is Sheila Mills's *Rocky Mountain Kettle Cuisine.*

The
Bedroom

IT HAS BEEN A LONG DAY of paddling, you're tired, and there's nothing like pulling into a warm, comfortable camp in the middle of a vast, unspoiled wilderness. A campsite, if you've taken the effort to select the right sleeping bag and tent, can be a place of respite, a virtual home away from home—and with a much better view.

SLEEPING BAGS

The sleeping bag is simple in concept, performing an unglamorous but invaluable function—it traps warm air to keep the body from cooling down at night. How well a sleeping bag performs this task is largely the result of its materials and its construction. Some familiarity with the terms of the technology may help you in picking the right bag.

Fill

The biggest factor in choosing a sleeping bag is the type of insulation (or "fill") that it's made of—either down (goose or duck) or synthetic. The ideal material would be lightweight, warm, compact, durable, quick-drying, and very soft. Unfortunately, the ideal fill doesn't exist, so a few compromises have to be made, depending upon when and where you camp, the shelter you use, and the chances of getting your bag wet.

Before DuPont launched Fiberfill II in the mid-'70s, synthetic-filled sleeping bags were far too heavy and bulky for canoeing. Since then, a host of good synthetic fills has appeared, and canoeists can now choose from a variety of lightweight and compact bags.

There are two basic types of synthetic fills: chopped fibers and continuous filaments. Chopped fibers are short sections of fill, often hollow inside. Continuous filaments are long strands of fiber. Polarguard is the only continuous filament, but there are many versions of chopped fibers, the best known being Quallofil and Hollofil II. Which is better matters less than the quality of the bag as a whole.

Synthetic fills cost less than down, are easy to care for, and resist moisture. The synthetics are not, however, entirely "warm when wet" as some manufacturers claim. Synthetic fills dry fairly quickly because they're nonabsorbent—an obvious advantage on a canoe trip. Because the fill doesn't collapse when saturated, much of its ability to trap warm air is retained. When compared to a wet down bag, a wet synthetic bag will start to feel warm in a short span of time, as long as it's protected from the wind. Compared to down, the disadvantages of synthetic fills are: a shorter life span, less comfort, more bulk, and greater weight.

The lightest, warmest, most comfortable, and most durable sleeping bags are those made of down. These bags are best when weight and bulk are critical, because no synthetic fiber has down's insulating ability.

Down has its disadvantages. It must be kept dry, as it loses virtually all its insulation when wet. It's also very absorbent, and it takes a long time to dry. Drying out a down bag in bad weather is almost impossible—only a hot sun or tumble dryer will do the job. Keeping the bag dry on a canoe trip means packing it in a completely waterproof bag (which is not that difficult with the new waterproof bags) and always taking shelter when it rains. Down bags also require frequent airing to remove moisture picked up from humid air or from your body during the night.

Down comes in different grades and types. Pure down is usually at least 85 percent down, the remainder being small feathers that are impossible to separate (the more stalks you feel, the higher the percentage of feathers in it). Goose down is regarded as warmer than duck down; it's also more expensive. The more space the down can fill, the higher its quality, as its thickness (or "loft") determines its warmth. The volume filled by 1 ounce of down gives a measurement called fill-power; most pure down has a fill-power of between 500 and 650 cubic inches per ounce.

Shell Materials

Nylon is the best material for containing the fill of a sleeping bag. It's lightweight, durable, wind- and water-resistant, nonabsorbent, and quick-drying. The latest nylons are comfortable against the skin, making them suitable for the inner as well as the outer shell. In the past, nylons felt cold and clammy, so many campers chose cotton or poly/cotton interiors, even though they're heavier, slower-drying, and harder to keep clean. The newest nylons, however, have a pleasant feel and the ability to spread moisture over the surface, which speeds up evaporation.

A breathable and waterproof outer shell (such as Gore-Tex) provides good water-resistance, but it adds to the weight and cost and will leak unless its seams are sealed. A few models come with special inner liners designed to increase warmth by reflecting back body heat.

Shape and Size

The most efficient bag is one that traps warm air close to the body—a roomy bag is one with lots of dead air space. Most bags reduce this dead space by tapering from head to foot, and they have hoods to prevent heat loss. The result is called a mummy bag, and it's the standard for high-performance sleeping bags used in cooler weather.

Many canoeists, however, object to the confines of a mummy bag, so they choose a semi-rectangular bag, which is warmer than a rectangular bag but less restricting than a mummy.

A sleeping bag that's too wide or too long won't keep you as warm as a bag that's the right size for you. At the other extreme, a bag that's too small won't keep you warm in spots where you press against the shell and flatten the fill.

Construction

The method used to hold fill in the sleeping bag determines how efficient the bag will be. Fill will migrate unless it's held in channels; to create these channels, the inner and outer shells of a bag are stitched together. The simplest way of doing this is sewn-through stitching, but heat escapes through the stitch lines, and the oval channels created don't allow the fill to expand fully.

To reduce this heat loss, the inner and outer shells can be connected by short walls of fabric to make boxes (called box-wall construction or slant-wall construction). Virtually all cold-weather down bags have these internal walls.

Synthetic bags can't use this construction because the fill is fixed in layers, so they use two other techniques. In double-layer construction, two (sometimes three) sewn-through layers are used, with the stitch lines offset to eliminate cold spots. In single-layer construction, slanted layers of overlapping fiber are sewn to both the inner and the outer shell. This is supposedly lighter and allows the fill to loft more easily.

Whatever the internal construction, a bag's channels are usually divided by lengthwise side baffles, which prevent the fill from ending up on the top or bottom of the bag. Some bags, usually light-weight down ones, dispense with side baffles on the theory that it might be useful at times to redistribute the fill. To prevent fill compression, the outer shell on many bags is cut larger than the inner; this is known as a differential cut.

Design

A good sleeping-bag hood will fit closely around the head, and it should have a drawcord with toggles to permit easy adjustment. Bags used in below-freezing temperatures usually have large hoods in which you can bury all but your nose. To prevent drafts, an insulated collar is often a feature. To keep your feet warm, a sleeping bag should have a shaped foot section; if the two halves of the bag are simply sewn together, your feet will compress the fill.

Zippers allow you to regulate temperature, and couples can zip two bags together to make one big bag. To prevent heat loss, zippers should have insulated baffles running down the inside.

Ratings

Rating sleeping bags for warmth is difficult, because there's no standard system. Most companies use ratings that give either the lowest temperature or a range in which the bag will be comfortable.

No rating system, however, can account for different metabolism rates. Some people are warm sleepers, some cold. Putting on more clothes is an obvious solution when you wake up in the night feeling chilled, but a carbohydrate snack can also help. If you camp without a tent, you'll need a warmer bag; using a sleeping pad also makes a big difference in both comfort and warmth.

Liners

Sleeping-bag liners are available in cotton, polypropylene, silk, pile, and coated nylon. Cotton is heavy and slow-drying; polypropylene liners, which absorb less moisture, make more sense. Pile liners, though bulky, can upgrade a bag for colder conditions, and silk is very light and compact.

Coated nylon liners can be used to form a vapor barrier that keeps in moisture and stops evaporative heat loss. In dry, cold conditions, especially when the temperature is well below freezing, a vapor-barrier liner (VBL) can add a surprising amount of warmth.

Care

In the field, all sleeping bags benefit from being aired out whenever possible. This is especially important with down bags, which absorb a surprising amount of moisture. Give down bags time to let their fill expand and a rigorous shake to ensure even distribution of the fill (these aren't necessary with synthetic bags).

Patch small holes in the fabric as soon as possible with adhesive-backed nylon to prevent fill from escaping. Although this is usually adequate, you can reinforce the first patch with a sewn one after you return home.

Never store down or synthetic bags compressed; eventually the fill won't expand fully. This affects synthetic bags most; prolonged compression renders the fill ineffective. Instead, bags should be stored flat, hung up, or inside a very large bag. To allow moisture to escape, they should not be stored in a waterproof bag.

No other maintenance is necessary until the bag requires cleaning. Synthetic bags can be machine-washed, though they shouldn't be dry-cleaned. Cleaning down-filled bags is a different matter. Because down loses some of its insulating properties every time it's cleaned, the bag should be cleaned only when the fill is so dirty it no longer keeps you warm.

The problem with cleaning down is that it absorbs water and the bag becomes very heavy. If the bag is lifted when wet, the baffles may tear. This is why down bags should be either dry-cleaned or carefully hand-washed in a bathtub. If hand-washed, the bag must be dried in a large tumble dryer to keep the down from forming clumps. Special soaps are needed, since standard detergents strip the natural oils from the down and thus shorten the bag's life.

If you choose to dry-clean your down bag, be sure to find an experienced cleaner; contact the store where you bought the bag for its recommendations. It's also important that the bag be well aired afterward to get rid of dry-cleaning fumes.

Pads and Pillows

For comfort and insulation, a sleeping bag needs a pad underneath it. There are basically two types: closed-cell and self-inflating. Air mattresses and open-cell foam are still available, but not as widely used. Closed-cell pads are light, reasonably cheap, and hardwearing, but they're bulky and don't add much padding. More comfortable is a self-inflating model such as the Therm-a-Rest, which has a nylon shell bonded to a core of open-cell foam that expands when the valve is opened (a few puffs speed up the process). The only problem with these pads is their slipperiness; to solve this, many campers buy pad covers or apply special sprays.

For a pillow, some canoeists use a pile or down jacket, perhaps packed into a stuffsack. If you prefer something more comfortable, there are a number of lightweight camp pillows available.

TENTS

Selecting the right tent isn't as easy as it might appear, since tents come in an almost limitless variety of shapes and sizes. Seek good advice from a salesperson and carefully study the outdoor gear catalogs. To narrow the field, you need to ask a few questions:

- When and where will it be used?
- How many must it sleep?
- How critical is weight?

Then, issues of price and personal choice come into play.

Because a tent's main purpose is to protect against wind and rain, it must be windproof and waterproof. It should also be lightweight and compact when packed, yet strong and durable to withstand severe weather.

Like rainwear, tents must repel rain while letting condensation escape. The moisture given off by the human body is considerable over the period of a night. The problem is minimized through the use of two layers—a breathable inner layer and a waterproof outer layer (or flysheet). Moisture passes through the inner fabric and is then carried away by the flow of air circulating between the two layers. Condensation occurs on the inside of the flysheet, where it runs to the ground.

Design

Since the advent of dome tents in the early '70s, designers have created a bewildering array of tent shapes, some of them quite elaborate. These developments have led to tents that are lighter, roomier, tougher, and more durable than ever.

DOME TENTS.

Before flexible tent poles appeared, all designs were variations on the standard ridge tent, a solid structure still popular with many canoeists. As good as traditional tents are, flexible-pole models are superior. Their steep sides and curved roofs give more usable space, and the self-supporting ones can be moved to a more suitable site after they've been erected.

Dome tents are those whose flexible poles cross each other at some point. They are the roomiest tents available, and most of them are self-supporting. There are two kinds: geodesic and crossover-

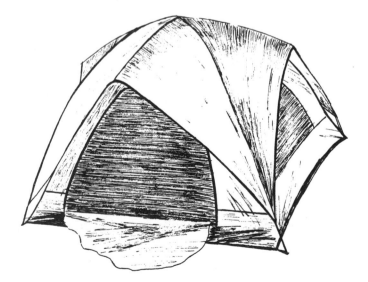

Dome tent

pole. Geodesic domes are complex structures with four or more poles that cross at several points. Crossover-pole domes have two or three poles that cross at the apex, creating a spacious tent lighter than but not as stable as the geodesic.

TRADITIONAL TENTS.

A lot of canoeists still prefer the traditional design of a large wall tent with its angled roof, often called an A-frame tent. One model has an entire side that can be opened (either with or without a mosquito netting). The advantages of this versatile tent are obvious: increased ventilation and better views. Many are made of canvas, rendering them fairly heavy and bulky.

Setting up the evening's shelter.

SIZE.

Tents come in a wide range of sizes. You'll want enough inner height to allow you to sit up and move around. You also need to consider the size of the tent's vestibule, if any. If you expect to cook and store gear there, it needs to be roomy.

Materials

Most tents are made of nylon or polyester, and these are undoubtedly the most practical. (Cotton canvas is heavy and absorbs moisture.) Nylon absorbs little moisture, dries quickly, and is very light. The flysheets used to cover most tents are plastic-coated to keep out rain. To prevent leaks, flysheet seams are often sealed with adhesive sealant, though some of the better ones come with fully taped seams.

Breathable fabrics can be used to combat condensation in tents as they do in clothing, and several models are made from Gore-Tex. These tents are easy to pitch because they have just one layer, but because the fabrics don't work well in larger tents, most models are small.

POLES.

Poles can be rigid or flexible. They're usually made from aluminum, though some are made from fiberglass. Poles with sections linked by elastic shockcord are the most convenient. Tents with solid poles should be avoided, because their unlinked sections tend to come apart inside the tent sleeves.

Most poles are attached to the tent by threading them through nylon or mesh sleeves and then fixing the end into a grommet strip or tape loop. A few models use clips or shockcord to hang the tent from the poles, which is faster to set up.

STAKES AND GUYLINES.

Regardless of its claims, every tent requires some staking to hold it down in strong winds. Long, heavy stakes aren't necessary. Smaller aluminum stakes hold in most soils; for softer ground, you can carry a few V-angle stakes. Stakes are easy to misplace, so take two or three extra.

Depending on design, tents need guylines to keep them taut in a wind. To avoid confusion, different-colored guylines may be useful, especially when several are attached to the tent at the same point. To tighten the guylines, sliders are handy.

Stability

For three-season, sheltered-site camping, stability is not a major concern. For exposed sites and cold-weather camping, it's a prime factor. The stability of a tent is determined by a host of factors—its shape, its materials, the number of poles and how they're arranged, and the number and position of its guylines. Look for a tent with plenty of guylines and no large areas of unsupported material.

Stability, of course, is relative. Violent gales can shred the strongest tent. In extreme winds, a sheltered site may be as important as your tent. When pitching the tent seems impossible because of high winds, it may be better to go on, even after dark, in search of a more protected spot.

The Closet

WHEN IT COMES TO CLOTHING, the experts agree: Buy the best and scrimp somewhere else. Your comfort in the wilds is too important to permit you to do otherwise. The prime purpose of clothing is to keep you warm and dry on the water, but it must also do the same in camp. With the new clothing designed specifically for camping, there's no reason to be wet and cold.

HEAT LOSS

It's easy for clothing to work if you're sitting still on a calm, dry day. But maintaining the body's temperature is difficult when you alternate sitting with varying degrees of activity in a range of temperatures and conditions. This is because an active body pumps out heat and moisture, which have to be dispersed. The body loses heat in four ways, and these determine how clothing must function:

CONVECTION.

Convection, the transfer of heat from the body to the air, is the major cause of heat loss. When air moves over the skin and through your clothing, it depletes warmth at an amazing rate. Clothing must reduce air flow over the skin; in other words, it must be windproof.

CONDUCTION.

Conduction is the transfer of heat from one surface to another. Air conducts heat poorly, so the best protection is clothing that traps and holds air. It's the still air that keeps you warm—the clothing just holds it in place.

EVAPORATION.

During vigorous exercise, the body gives off as much as a quart of water an hour. Clothing must transport it away quickly so that it doesn't absorb body heat. Wearing garments that can be ventilated easily, especially at the neck, is important.

RADIATION.

This is the passing of heat between two objects without warming the intervening space. Radiation requires a direct pathway, so wearing tightly woven clothing helps reduce the loss of body heat.

LAYERING

The usual solution to the clothing dilemma is to wear several light layers of clothing on the torso and arms (the legs require less protection). These layers can then be adjusted to suit the prevailing conditions and your level of activity. Layering is versatile and efficient if used properly, which means constantly opening and closing zippers and cuff fastenings, and occasionally stopping to remove or put on clothes.

A typical layering wardrobe consists of an inner layer of thin material to remove moisture from the skin, a thicker midlayer to trap air and provide insulation, and an outer shell to keep off wind and rain while allowing perspiration to pass through. A basic three-layer system includes a synthetic undershirt; a pile, fleece, or wool layer; and a breathable, waterproof shell.

To this may be added a synthetic, wool, or cotton shirt or sweater, and perhaps a down- or synthetic-insulation-filled garment if it's really cold. If the weather is wet as well as cold, another pile or fleece jacket can substitute for the insulation-filled garment.

How many layers you take depends on the conditions you expect. You should, of course, take clothing that will keep you warm in the worst weather you're likely to encounter. If in doubt, take a light down- or synthetic-insulated vest, just in case.

INNER LAYER

Often described as "thermal" underwear, this layer keeps the skin *dry* rather than warm. If perspiration is quickly removed from the skin's surface, it's easier for the outer layer to keep you warm. Conversely, if the layer next to your skin becomes saturated and dries slowly, your other clothes, no matter how good, will have a hard time keeping you warm. No fabric, regardless of its claims, is warm when wet.

While on the move, you can stay warm even if your inner layers are damp, as long as your outer layer keeps out rain and wind and your midlayer provides some warmth. But once you stop, wet underwear will chill you rapidly. Once you stop exercising, your heat output drops rapidly, just when you need it to dry out your wet underwear.

The material to avoid at all costs is cotton, because it absorbs moisture quickly and takes a long time to dry. To make matters worse, it clings to the skin, preventing a dry layer of air from forming.

Fabrics remove moisture in two ways. They either transport or "wick" moisture away from the skin and into the air (or into the next layer of clothing), or they absorb it before slowly passing it to the other side. Wicking is accomplished through specially developed synthetic materials, while traditional, natural fibers absorb moisture.

You may have to wear undergarments for days without washing them, so they must work for a long time and, ideally, not absorb odors. Some of the synthetics come in heavier weights for colder conditions, but they don't wick moisture as fast as the lighter-weight versions.

Designs are simple: short- and long-sleeved crewneck tops, long-sleeved zip-neck tops, and long pants. Close-fitting garments wick moisture quicker, and they allow midlayers to fit easily over them. Wrist and ankle cuffs need to grip well to keep them from riding up. Seams should be flat-sewn (not raised) to avoid rubbing and abrasion. Dark colors are best because dirt and stains show up less. Check the laundering instructions: Underwear requiring special care should be avoided.

Choosing a synthetic fabric for underwear can be difficult because there are so many brands, all claiming to work best. The three main choices are polypropylene, polyester, and PVC:

POLYPROPYLENE.

Polypropylene is the lightest and thinnest of these fabrics. Polypro won't absorb moisture, but instead wicks it along its fibers and into the air or the next layer. When you stop exercising, it wicks away your sweat so fast that after-exercise chill is negligible. However, polypro absorbs odors and doesn't smell fresh after a day or so, and it shrinks when washed in hot water. If you don't wash it every couple of days, it ceases to work properly. As a result, you have to carry several garments or rinse out one regularly. Newer versions of polypro have a softer, less "plastic" feel, and they can be washed at higher temperatures.

POLYESTER.

Polyester repels water but has a low wicking ability. However, it can be treated chemically so the surface absorbs water while the core repels it; the result is that moisture spreads over the material and quickly dries. Most versions contain antibacterial treatment to prevent odor buildup. Unlike polypro, it can be washed at relatively high temperatures.

PVC.

Like polypro and polyester, polyvinyl chloride (PVC) absorbs little water and wicks well. It's comfortable and efficient, but shrinks drastically if put in more than lukewarm water. PVC isn't as bad as old-style polypro, but it retains body odor after a few days' wear. For strength, it's usually blended with nylon or polyester in an 80:20 mix.

WOOL.

Wool, the traditional material, is not as popular as it once was, yet it has much to recommend it. Rather than rapidly wicking moisture, wool works more slowly, absorbing moisture to leave a dry surface against the skin. Relatively lightweight, it can absorb up to 35 percent of its weight in water before it feels wet and cold. Once wet, it's slow to dry. Many people, however, find it to be too itchy. Wool's other limitation is its warmth, which makes it suitable only for colder weather.

SILK.

Silk is the other natural material used in outdoor underwear. It can absorb up to 30 percent of its weight without feeling damp, so it feels warm when wet. It's light, too, though its best attribute is its luxurious feel. But it doesn't dry quickly, and it has to be hand-washed and dried flat.

MIDLAYER

This is the layer that traps air and keeps you warm. Midlayer clothing has to deal with the body moisture it receives from the inner layer, so it must either wick that moisture away or absorb it without losing its insulation.

Midlayer clothing comes in every design imaginable: shirts, sweaters, anoraks, and jackets. High collars will keep your neck warm and hold in heat, while garments that open down the front are easier to ventilate than crewneck ones. There are a number of materials to choose from:

SYNTHETIC THERMAL.

You can wear two layers of thin thermal underwear, but most manufacturers offer it in heavier versions, which make good midlayers.

WOOL AND COTTON.

The traditional alternative to a synthetic fabric is wool or cotton. Wool is heavy, bulky, and takes forever to dry. Cotton, too, is heavy and dries slowly. Both have become less attractive when compared to pile and fleece.

PILE AND FLEECE.

Pile and fleece insulate well, wick moisture quickly, and are lightweight, hard-wearing, warm when wet, and fast-drying. This makes them ideal for canoe camping.

There are many different types and weights of pile and fleece. *Pile* generally describes a loosely knit fabric with a furry surface, while *fleece* is tightly knitted and has a smooth finish. Manufacturers don't always use these terms consistently. Most piles and fleeces are made from polyester, though a few are made from nylon; neither has any particular advantages over the other.

Worn over a synthetic inner layer and under a breathable waterproof shell, a pile/fleece top will keep you warm in just about any weather. Pile is most effective in cold, wet conditions, in which other materials don't work well. A pile top can wick moisture almost as fast as synthetic underwear. If you feel cold, nothing will keep you as warm as a pile top, even a damp one.

Pile does have its drawbacks. Most garments are not windproof, which means you need a shell over them, even in a cool breeze. They can be worn over a wide temperature range—without a shell when it's warm or calm, and with one when it's cold or windy. Shelled jackets are available, but they're heavier, bulkier, and not as versatile. Pile's biggest disadvantage is that it doesn't compress well.

Pile garments need to be close-fitting to trap warm air efficiently and to wick moisture away quickly. They're prone to the bellows effect, in which cold air sucked in at the bottom of the garment replaces warm air. So the hem should be elasticized or have a drawcord. Wrist cuffs work best if they're close-fitting, as do neck closures. The broad, stretchy ribbing found on the cuffs and hems of many jackets works well, but it absorbs moisture and takes a long time to dry; the nonabsorbent and quick-drying Lycra is better.

Most pile garments are hip-length, which is just about right. A high collar will help keep your neck warmer, and low, hand-warming pockets are useful.

INSULATED CLOTHING.

When a pile/fleece garment won't keep you warm on its own, you need an additional insulating layer. This garment could be a second, perhaps thicker, pile one, but many campers prefer down-filled clothing, which is warmer than pile, more compact, and more windproof.

Down is still the lightest, warmest insulation there is, and it provides more warmth for its weight than pile. Down, however, must be kept dry: When it's wet, it loses its insulating ability, and it dries very slowly.

If you're allergic to feathers or worried about garments that won't work when wet, consider high-loft polyester-filled jackets. They're cold when wet, but they dry quickly. They are, however, bulkier than pile and down garments.

The alternative to polyester is the thin microfiber insulations that dominate skiwear because of their slim looks. First in the field was Thinsulate, and there are now others. They're made from very fine polyester and polypropylene fibers that trap more air than any other material, including down. They are, however, bulky to pack, and they dry more slowly than pile and fleece.

OUTER LAYER

If the outer layer fails, it doesn't matter how good your inner garments are. Wet clothing exposed to the wind is chilly regardless of the material it's made from. The choices in the materials for your outer layer are between breathable and nonbreathable fabrics.

BREATHABLE FABRICS.

The moisture given off by your body eventually reaches the outer layer. If it can't escape, it condenses on the inner surface of the rain shell and eventually soaks back into your clothes. The solution is fabrics that allow water vapor to pass through while keeping the rain out. These breathable fabrics are referred to as moisture-vapor-permeable (MVP); the best-known is Gore-Tex.

Since the advent of Gore-Tex, a number of waterproof fabrics claiming to transmit moisture vapor have appeared. Breathable garments need to be close-fitting to keep the air inside as warm as possible, because this enables the fabric to work more effectively. However, opening the front or undoing wrist fastenings is still the quickest and most efficient way to vent moisture.

Breathable fabrics aren't perfect, of course: There's a limit to the amount of moisture even the best can transmit in a given time. This means that when you exert yourself and perspire heavily, you won't be completely dry, nor will you be so in a continuously heavy rain. When the outside of any garment is running with water, breathability is reduced and condensation forms. In a nonbreathable garment, condensation forms until you take it off, so you stay wet even after it's stopped raining. With the best breathable fabrics, once your activity slows down and you produce less moisture, any dampness will dry out through the fabric. The same happens after a heavy rain.

There are two categories of breathable materials: coatings and laminates. Coatings are layers of waterproofing (usually polyurethane) applied to a base fabric (usually nylon). Laminates are a sandwich of materials, the key layer of which is a very thin, waterproof, breathable membrane.

Coated fabrics, such as Entrant, are popular, with new ones appearing. None breathe as well as the laminates, but they're an improvement over nonbreathable coatings and the best ones work very well indeed.

Laminates, such as Gore-Tex, are the most effective (and most expensive) breathable fabrics. Their microporous membrane can be laminated to a range of fabrics, mostly nylons, though sometimes polyester or poly/cotton. The thicker the fabric, the more durable the garment, but the lower its breathability. In three-layer laminates, the membrane is glued between two layers of nylon to produce a hard-wearing, though somewhat stiff, material. More breathable, but less durable, are two-layer laminates (in which the membrane is stuck to an outer layer and the inner lining hangs free) and drop liners (in which the membrane is left loose between an inner and an outer layer).

NONBREATHABLE FABRICS.

This rain gear is made from nylon coated with polyurethane or neoprene. Polyurethane is cheaper than neoprene, but eventually cracks and peels. Neoprene is extremely hard-wearing. Both will leave you soaked in sweat after exercising; the only way to remove that moisture is to ventilate the jacket, which is hardly practical if it's pouring.

While moving, you'll still feel warm, even if your undergarments are wet with sweat, because nonbreathable rainwear holds in heat with the moisture. Because rain is colder than perspiration, it's better to wear a nonbreathable waterproof shell than a breathable nonwaterproof one. When you stop, though, you'll cool down rapidly unless you put on dry clothes.

Design

Material alone is not enough to ensure that a garment is waterproof. Design is almost as crucial: The better the ventilation, the less condensation there will be. The two basic choices are between zippered and pullover garments. Heavy wind-driven rain will find its way into any garment if given enough time. The best will keep out most precipitation most of the time—that's about all you can ask.

Length is a matter of personal choice. Hip-length garments will give your legs greater freedom of movement, but many people prefer longer, even knee-length ones (called cagoules), so they don't have to resort to rain pants as often.

Seams are critical for ensuring maximum waterproofness. In breathable garments and the more expensive nonbreathable ones, the seams are tape-sealed. In cheaper garments, they may be coated with sealant instead. If you have a garment with uncoated seams,

Cagoule

or if the sealant wears off, you can buy the sealant and coat them yourself.

The front zipper is the other major source of leakage. This must be covered with a single (or preferably a double) waterproof flap, closed with either snaps or Velcro. Even with this, water may eventually find its way in. Often it's at the neck, which a high collar helps prevent.

Hoods are potential leak points. Good ones fit closely around the face when the drawcords are tightened, and the best ones move with your head. A stiffened peak helps keep off driving rain, and those who wear glasses find them essential. The hood should be big enough to allow a warm cap to be worn underneath it.

Sleeves must be cut full under the arms to allow for free movement and to keep them from riding up. Some garments have underarm zippers; they allow for better ventilation but tend to leak in heavy rain. The cuffs should be adjustable: Simple external Velcro-closed cuffs are preferred over the more awkward internal storm cuffs; nonadjustable elasticized ones will make your arms overheat.

Pockets are undoubtedly useful, but making them waterproof is difficult. Pocket openings should be covered by flaps, and seams should be taped or sealed on the inside. The most water-resistant pockets hang inside the jacket, attached only at the top. An advantage of pullover garments is that they usually have a single large "kangaroo" pouch on the chest, which is easy to use and very water-resistant.

Rain Pants

Rain pants should have adjustable waists, and the zippers in the lower leg should be long enough to allow you to pull them on without taking off your boots or shoes. If the zippers have gussets behind them, they'll keep out more water, but the zippers may catch on them. Full-length two-way zippers are useful because the pants can be ventilated by unzipping them from the waist down to the knee.

Hats

The array of hats used on canoe outings is indescribable. But there's a purpose here: An amazingly large amount of heat—anywhere from 20 to 75 percent—can be lost if the head is uncovered. The capillaries of the head don't close down to conserve heat the way they do in hands and feet. The old adage, "If you want warm feet, put on a hat," is true.

Headnets

For mosquito-ridden campsites, these are a necessity. Also available, for the worst conditions, are mosquito-netted suits that are saturated in repellent.

Footwear

Footwear around the campsite varies. A lot of campers simply wear the shoes or sandals they've had on the water, as long as they're dry. Others choose lightweight hiking boots. Still others prefer the comfort of that Native American classic, the moccasin.

Gloves

Many campers like to have lightweight cotton or leather gloves for handling firewood and other chores around camp. If the weather's cold, a pair of wool, pile, or insulated gloves is better.

Bandannas

An ordinary bandanna can be used for a variety of purposes—scarf, hat, headband, towel, water filter, bandage, sling, distress signal.

LIFE JACKETS

Few pieces of boating gear have progressed more in comfort and safety than the life jacket. The "Personal Flotation Devices," as they're called by the Coast Guard, that are suitable for canoeing fall into two categories: Type III and Type V. Type III Buoyant Devices are thinner and more comfortable to wear, but provide less flotation, than Type V, which are designed specifically for whitewater use. (Incidentally, Type I is the bulky orange "Mae West" jacket filled with Kapok; Type II is the horse-collar version, which is inadequate for river use; and Type IV is a buoyant seat cushion, which is unsuitable for just about everything.)

When choosing a PFD, favor safety over comfort. The amount of flotation you require in a life jacket depends on your body's own buoyancy, your experience, and the water you'll be tackling. For lakes and easy rivers, a "shortie" Type III offers a good measure of safety and the advantage of unrestricted motion. In big whitewater, a Type V or a "high-flotation" version of the Type III is better. There should be sufficient buckles and straps to secure the jacket firmly about your body. You'll want to wear the PFD snugly to keep it from riding up over your head, so make certain you buy a jacket that fits well. Most Type IIIs are sold by chest size, while the majority of Type Vs are "one size fits all" and require more adjustments. Fit is important to safety, especially for children and smaller adults.

Always fasten *all* the buckles, zippers, and waist ties when you put the jacket on—*never* wear the PFD loose or open in the front.

And pull the side adjustment-straps down snugly and secure them. This is also important to avoid entangling yourself should the boat overturn. Make a habit, too, of fastening your life jacket down when you take it off in camp, so the wind doesn't blow it away.

A good PFD will give you years of protection if treated properly. Don't use your life jacket as a seat cushion. After each trip, hang the jacket to maintain its shape and to prevent it from mildewing. Clean it often, following the manufacturer's instructions, using a mild soap so as not to harm the interior foam.

Camping Accessories

A LOT OF CANOE CAMPERS try to take everything with them—and I do mean *everything*. The beauty is that the canoe can accommodate most of their desires. Other canoeists are less inclined toward taking it all, though they still like to pack those things that make them comfortable in their home away from home.

WATERPROOF BAGS

When you arrive in camp, you'll want your gear—especially your sleeping bag and clothes—to be dry. The quality and variety of waterproof bags on the market has improved dramatically. A number of relatively inexpensive PVC bags made just for river runners are now available, and many are very reliable; more expensive, but exceptionally durable, are those bags made out of neoprene and Hypalon. Many of these bags have backpacker-style shoulder straps, which are convenient in portaging and moving your gear to camp.

A less expensive alternative is to place a heavy-duty plastic bag inside a more durable nylon bag. Canoeists have used this arrangement for years, but it's critical that the seal on the plastic bag be secure.

Modern waterproof bag

The traditional waterproofing system—and one still used by many Boundary Waters trippers—is the Duluth pack, developed in 1882 and manufactured by the Duluth Pack Company for the past eighty-five years. It's made of rugged canvas and has leather backpack straps. There are a number of models specifically made for carrying food and kitchen gear. These bags are heavier, but will last for generations. A newer version is made of nylon, which some people prefer. With these bags, you'll need to add a plastic inner liner if you expect to encounter any whitewater.

A good waterproof bag, properly treated, will last for years. Always carry the bag, and avoid dragging it over sand and rocks. If you transport the bag on a roof rack, be careful that the loading straps don't chafe the bag.

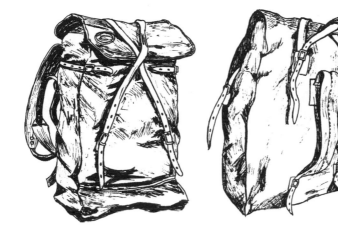

Duluth pack

WATERPROOF BOXES

Waterproof boxes of various kinds are used by canoeists to carry food, kitchen equipment, cameras, and a host of other gear. The traditional wooden box, often handmade, is called the wanigan. Many are quite elaborate, with shelves and compartments. The degree of waterproofing varies, making some suitable only for kitchen equipment and canned goods.

More modern versions include a plastic backpack-like container complete with straps. There are also large plastic containers that are cavernous and fill up most of a canoe. Many

Wanigan

Modern waterproof box

Pack basket

canoeists prefer the old military surplus ammunition boxes, which come in a variety of sizes. The larger models are well suited for food and kitchen supplies, while the smaller ones make excellent camera cases.

The traditional hard-shell container for canoeing is the pack basket, made of strips of wood woven together. These are typically placed inside a Duluth pack or lined with a plastic bag. They're beautiful pieces, recalling a bygone era of voyageurs in the North Country.

TARPS

Some canoeists use tarps for shelter in an attempt to cut down on their load. This works fine if the weather—and mosquitoes—allow it. Even those who take tents find a tarp useful for shade in midday or for a dining canopy at night. A number of models are made in sophisticated, geometric designs that look attractive and shed the wind nicely. The key to a good tarp setup is lots of nylon line.

LIGHTS

Unless you're camping near the Arctic Circle, you'll probably need some kind of area light. The Coleman lantern comes to mind because it has been used for generations: Many canoeists wouldn't use anything else. Most lanterns work on white gas, though there are propane and battery-operated models available. The amount of light provided is astonishing.

Those looking for a lightweight alternative have a choice of identical lanterns, only smaller. An even more compact option is the candle lantern, though the amount of light given off is considerably less.

For directional light, there's an almost limitless variety of flashlights in a variety of sizes. Many canoeists prefer headlamps, which leave hands free for cooking and other tasks. Carrying spare batteries and bulbs is always a good idea.

LOUNGE CHAIRS

Even the purists have now come to recognize the benefits of a camp chair, and its use has become almost ubiquitous among canoe campers. The design of these chairs has become quite sophisticated, and many are so light that weight and bulk are hardly an issue. A

Nothing beats a lawn chair for relaxing by the water.

number of the recliner models are so comfortable they verge on the decadent.

CAMP SHOWERS

This is another invention that has encouraged canoe camping among those who miss their luxuries back home. No longer is it necessary to forgo a hot shower simply because you're in the wilderness. Leave the shower (typically black plastic) in the sun all day, and the results that evening are magic. Highly recommended.

WATER BUCKETS

A number of collapsible water buckets are now available, and they serve well in hauling water to camp and as dishwashing buckets. Choose the sturdier models for reliability.

TOOLS

In this department are knives, axes, saws, shovels, and a number of other ingenious tools. The ax, saw, and shovel are an important part of canoe camping lore, and a lot of people carry them for that reason alone. Even with the compact models designed for camping, many canoeists find their use too rare to justify taking them. It's a matter of choice.

Knives are obviously important for the kitchen, where most campers prefer a sheath knife because of its size and convenience. A lot of campers pack along a folding knife as well, especially those of the Swiss Army variety with their infinite variety of screwdrivers, files, magnifying glasses, and so forth.

The latest development is the multitool, such as the Leatherman, which contains pliers, knife blades, files, screwdrivers, and wire cutter in one compact package. Regardless of how often they're used, they look good strapped to your belt.

SUNGLASSES

When you're camping on a stretch of water, glare is a frequent problem. Sunglasses can help relieve much of the discomfort, and even potential damage, to your eyes. Unfortunately, not all models do the job equally well. A good pair of sunglasses will reduce light to a comfortable level, but equally important, they must decrease ultraviolet and infrared radiation.

Optical experts agree that a good pair of sunglasses should provide 15 to 35 percent light transmission. Therefore, the lenses should absorb 65 to 85 percent of the rays striking them. Ultraviolet and infrared transmission should be at least as low.

The manufacturer of the sunglasses you're considering should provide these specifications. If it doesn't, a rough method of determining visible light transmission is to look in a mirror. Lenses through which the eyes are easily visible are probably too light for proper glare protection.

Almost all lenses block some ultraviolet, but not all control infrared. Unless the manufacturer provides this information, the buyer's safest investment is green or gray sunglasses, which are most likely to provide sufficient protection. They also provide the best color perception, because the human eye is sensitive to these wavelengths.

Mirrored sunglasses have a thin coating of steel alloy that reflects light off the front of the lenses, providing greater protection without the necessity for darker lenses. The drawback is that they can increase sunburn of the nose.

Polarizing lenses eliminate glare from flat surfaces. But viewing objects from other angles diminishes the effect: At 90 degrees, virtually no glare is eliminated. This makes them a questionable investment.

Photochromic lenses, which automatically darken as the light increases, are designed to increase eye protection as the intensity of ultraviolet light increases. But they absorb few infrared rays.

Still another category is mountaineering sunglasses, which have extremely dark lenses and leather side shields. Use caution when selecting them: Their darkness may result in pupil dilation and thereby actually *increase* the UV transmission to the eyes.

BINOCULARS

It's amazing how few campers take binoculars, and yet how often they express regret about it. Their usefulness, it seems, is frequent—for identifying birds, spotting mountain sheep, even determining whether to pull over for the day because the last campsite downstream has been taken.

Perhaps people think that binoculars are expensive (and some undoubtedly are), but in reality the price range is wide, with several good models costing less than a good rainsuit. Perhaps the descriptive jargon, such as *focal lengths* and *complex prisms*, sounds too complicated (though the basic specifications can be mastered in minutes).

Most binocular literature refers to two numbers: "7 x 35," for example. The first of the numbers, the "7" here, refers to the magnification of the object. You would think the greater the magnification, the better, but the slightest hand tremor can distort the image of binoculars with a power of, say, greater than 7 or 8. Generally, too, the greater the magnification, the narrower the field of view.

The second number, the "35" here, refers to the diameter of the front lenses in millimeters. The greater the number, the more light that's allowed to enter. But bigger is not necessarily better; unless you need night vision, there's little advantage in having a lens diameter greater than five times that of magnification. A number of good models have a factor of three (such as 8 x 24).

Obviously, the binoculars you choose should be light, compact, comfortable, and, most of all, water-resistant. Prices will be determined by lens quality, coatings, and prism setups. Some operating features will vary: Some users prefer center focusing (allowing quick refocusing at short range, which is best for birdwatching), while others like the individual focusing of each eyepiece (which is said to be more durable). Even wide-angle binoculars are available. The number of models on the market is overwhelming, and with a little research, you shouldn't have any trouble finding what you're looking for.

OTHER GEAR

A few other items that most campers like to bring along:

CAMERAS.

The choice is wide, and a number of rugged, compact models designed specifically for camping are available.

FISHING GEAR.

A lot of canoeists are just anglers in disguise. The variety of compact rods and reels for backcountry travel is impressive.

FIELD GUIDES.

The more you know about the flora and fauna of an area, the more you'll appreciate it.

HIKING BOOTS.

Hiking is one of camping's best diversions, and many canoe campers bring along a pair of lightweight hiking boots for hitting the trail.

PACK TOWEL.

This ingenious camping device serves as a bath towel, but is so absorbent it's a fraction of the size. It's also extremely quick-drying.

COMPASSES.

These are handy for side hikes and for following your route on a topographic map. Also useful are the map wheels that give distance.

GAMES.

Speaking of diversions, there are now board games made for canoeists looking to while away the evening hours spent sitting around the campfire, or inside a tent during a rainstorm.

MUSICAL INSTRUMENTS.

Flutes, kazoos, and even larger musical instruments can be brought along to provide entertainment at night.

BOOKS.

More than likely, you'll be too busy, but should you get stuck in a storm, it's nice to have something to read.

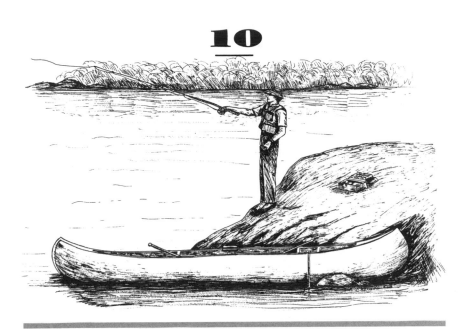

10

Wilderness Living

TO THE UNINITIATED, even the word *wilderness* has an intimidating feel to it. But a little knowledge and experience soon dispel the fears. Nature, of course, has its rough edges, but time spent among its unspoiled beauty is clearly one of life's finest pleasures.

WEATHER WATCHING

It's a great day on the river, with the sun shining, birds chirping, fish jumping, and all that, and then suddenly—everything breaks loose. As the gale-driven front bullies its way across the gray horizon, you find yourself paddling frantically to shore and running for cover, where you spend the day in a tent whose walls seem to compress as the day drags on.

If weather is anything, it's unpredictable. For that reason alone, it's important to be mindful of weather not only in the planning of a trip, but also once you're on the water. A good understanding of its volatile nature helps you not only in choosing the right clothing to pack, but also in attending to such health and safety matters as rising water levels and the prevention of hypothermia (and perhaps heatstroke as well).

A canoeist, like a professional meteorologist, has a number of weapons in his or her weather-predicting arsenal. Information about past conditions—monthly tables of previous temperatures, relative humidity, average rainfall, days without rain, and so forth—is helpful in the planning stages of a river trip. Ranging from a month before the trip until the day you leave, the forecasts on the Weather Channel are an invaluable aid in making decisions on what camping gear and clothing you should take.

Additionally, there's the in-the-field forecasting that inevitably comes while you're on the water. A casual forecast of "Certainly looks like rain to me" is sure to be countered with a more skeptical "I really don't think *that* cloud has any moisture in it." Obviously, there's nothing you can do to affect the weather, but the forces above should be observed because they can have an impact on your plans.

The border between two air masses is known as a front, and the interactions between them are determined by the weight of the air. Cold, dry air is heavy; warm, moist air is light. These different weights cause variations in air pressures—the highs and the lows that weathermen are always talking about. In simplest terms, rain and snow are just condensation that occurs when a warm, moist air mass rides over a heavy, cold one.

Logically enough, a front is deemed warm if the warmer sub-tropical air is advancing, and cold if the cold polar air is gaining ground. Most large storms are the result of what is known as an occluded front, which results when two fast-moving, cold air masses meet, restricting the warm air in size and lifting it completely off the ground.

Clouds are telltale signs of an imminent change in weather. If interpreted correctly, they can inform you about upper wind drifts, precipitation levels, instability of fronts, and the speed of oncoming changes in weather. Clouds are convection currents made visible when the dew point is reached. The main cloud formations are the big, wispy *cirrus;* the layered *stratus;* and the massive *cumulus.* The terms *alto,* meaning "high," and *nimbus,* meaning "rain," further describe their formations.

The massy, mountainlike cumulus clouds (and in particular the altocumulus clouds with their globular cloudlets that look like white paving stones) are the forerunners of a cold front, especially when followed by lower, denser clouds. They require immediate attention because they appear only a few hours before a storm, thus giving little advance warning. However, the disturbance is usually short-lived.

The thin and wispy cirrus clouds, appearing like curls of hair extremely high in the air, are the earliest signs of an approaching warm front, usually giving plenty of warning time, since they precede the front and its storm by eighteen to thirty-six hours. When these cirrus clouds merge into layered stratus (and especially the lower and darker cirrostratus), a storm is almost assured.

What are the best warnings of an impending storm? The experts give three: (1) shifts in wind speed and direction, (2) changes in the sky's appearance, and (3) variations in temperature, humidity, and pressure. As it turns out, the experts' advice is often consistent with the homey folklore.

The adage of "red sky at night, sailor's delight" is sometimes misleading, but that of "red sky at morning, sailor's warning" is generally reliable. The movement of upper clouds tells the direction of the winds aloft; if it's greatly different from the winds below, a change in weather is usually in the cards.

Another accurate aid in from-the-hip forecasting is wind direction. As a general rule, if the wind is from the north or west, it means you're on the east side of an eastward-moving high-pressure area (away from the front), and fair weather is probable for the next several days. On the other hand, if the wind is from the east or south, you're on the east side of an eastward-moving low-pressure area (near the front), and wet conditions are likely. Because winds from any direction generally die down at night, any persistent or strong winds after sundown usually indicate that stormy weather is on its way.

Other weather folklore is contradictory, and some downright bizarre. Leaving aside weather indicators related to insect behavior, arthritis, and even corns on the feet, some of the most common, but least trustworthy, has to do with phases and shapes of the moon. More reliable is the presence of a ring or halo around the moon or sun, formed by refraction through ice crystals in the clouds. These cirrostratus clouds are often seen when rain is approaching in less than twenty-four hours, but because these rings are also visible in rainless weather, they do give false alarms.

For further reading. A good reference for in-the-field forecasters is *Basic Essentials of Weather Forecasting*, by Michael Hodgson.

DEALING WITH ANIMALS

Encountering animals in the wilderness, even hazardous ones, is not usually a cause for alarm. In fact, observing wildlife at close quarters is one of the joys of wilderness travel.

We're intruders in these animals' world, so it's important not to approach or disturb them. When you come across animals unexpectedly and at close quarters, it's best to move away slowly and quietly. With most animals, you need fear attack only if you startle a mother with her young, and even then, as long as you back off, the chances are good that nothing will happen.

The river provides the perfect venue for wildlife watching.

Snakes

Snakes are probably more feared than any other animal, yet most species are harmless and the chances of being bitten are remote. Even those who are bitten are unlikely to be seriously harmed, unless the snake is a coral snake or a rattlesnake.

Bites rarely occur above the ankle, so wearing boots and thick socks in snake country minimizes the chances. Snakes are creatures of the night, so don't walk around barefooted or in sandals after dark.

A small snakebite kit containing a suction cup and a scalpel is one precaution. The current advice is *not* to use such kits because an untrained person can cause more harm than the bite itself. It's suggested instead that you wash the bite thoroughly with soap and water. Then bandage tightly over the bite around the entire limb, splint it, and keep it hanging down to reduce the amount of venom entering the bloodstream. The victim should rest while someone goes for assistance. If you're too far from help, you may have to sit out a day or two feeling very ill. For more information, consult *Medicine for Mountaineering* by James A. Wilkerson.

Bears

If you're in bear country, there are several steps you can take to minimize the chances of an encounter. Food in camp may attract bears (see the bear-proofing discussion in chapter 5). When you're on the move, you want bears to know you're there. Most of the time, their senses of smell and hearing will alert them long before you're aware of them. However, a wind blowing, a noisy stream, or thick brush can conceal you, so many people wear bells, shout and sing, clap their hands, or blow a safety whistle.

Be alert for signs of bears. Paw prints and piles of dung are obvious indications, but look for scratch marks on trees and mounds of freshly dug earth in meadows, where they've been digging for rodents.

If you see a bear before it sees you, detour quietly and quickly away from it. Be particularly wary of female grizzlies with cubs, as most attacks are made by mothers defending their young. If the bear is aware of you, move away from it, waving your arms or talking to help it identify what you are. Don't stare at it or act aggressively. In wooded country, look for a tree to climb as you move away. Black bears can climb trees but may not follow you, and the more dangerous grizzly can't climb, though it can reach amazingly high when standing on its back legs.

Occasionally, a grizzly will charge. Advice is mixed about what to do. It's worth climbing a tree if one is close—you can't outrun a bear. Dropping an object, such as a camera or piece of clothing, may serve as a distraction and allow you to escape. If that doesn't work, the choices are: trying to frighten the bear by yelling; banging objects together (metal on metal may be effective); backing away slowly; acting nonthreateningly by talking quietly to the bear; and as a last resort dropping to the ground in a fetal position and playing dead (covering the back of your neck with your hands).

You could also use a strong version of cayenne pepper sprays, which have been shown to repel bears. They aren't, however, a substitute for knowing about bear behavior and taking the usual precautions. If you're going to be in bear country, good books on the subject are *Bear Attacks: Their Causes and Avoidance,* by Stephen Herrero, and *Safe Travel in Bear Country,* by Gary Brown.

Insects

If you're unprepared, swarms of mosquitoes or no-see-ums can drive you crazy. Preparation means insect repellent, though dressing carefully can also help. You can cover up with tightly woven, light-colored clothing (dark colors attract some insects) and perhaps even wear a headnet. Fasten wrist and ankle cuffs tightly. The most effective repellent is diethyltoluamide (DEET for short), the active ingredient in most repellents. DEET turns plastics pliable so keep it well away from pocketknife handles, cameras, and the like.

Sustained use of DEET may also be harmful to the skin. It shouldn't be used at all by children or for long periods by adults. One alternative is to use repellent with a more diluted concentration of DEET, say, 25 to 50 percent, which is almost as effective as the stronger solutions. Non-DEET alternatives and oil of citronella, a traditional insect repellent, are also available. Burning a mosquito coil or citronella candle will also help keep insects at bay. Other suggestions include massive doses of vitamin B and garlic.

Ticks are usually no more than an irritant, but they can carry fatal diseases. Two of the better-known tick-borne diseases are Rocky Mountain spotted fever (found mainly in the East, despite the name) and Lyme disease. Fortunately, both can be cured with antibiotics. Symptoms of Rocky Mountain spotted fever include fatigue and loss of appetite. These soon develop into a fever and a red rash on the hands and feet. If untreated, the disease lasts for several weeks and is fatal in 20 to 30 percent of cases.

Lyme disease also appears within a few weeks of the bite and often involves a red rash, this time a circular one. It isn't fatal, but if it's not treated, it can recur and later lead to severe arthritis.

A sensible precaution is to check for ticks when you're in areas where they're endemic, especially in late spring and early summer. Ticks live in grasses and leaves, so care should be taken in thick undergrowth. Wearing long clothing helps, as does applying repellent to cuffs and ankles. Ticks embedded in the skin can be removed by touching them with antiseptic (they then withdraw their mouth-pieces), and picking them off with tweezers.

POISONOUS PLANTS

A few poisonous plants—such as poison oak, poison ivy, and poison sumac—can cause you discomfort. They often cause severe allergic reactions, and if you brush against these plants, you should immediately scrub the affected area with soap and water. You should also wash any clothing or equipment that has come into contact with them. If you start to itch, try calamine lotion, cool salt-water compresses, or cortisone creams.

SUNSCREEN

Protecting your skin with sunscreen is a necessity on canoe trips, where the glare from the water intensifies the sun's rays. Of the many sunscreens on the market, choose those that don't wash off as quickly with water and sweat. All sunscreens have a sun protection factor (SPF) number; the higher the SPF, the more protection. SPFs of 15 and above provide virtually total protection and are recommended for high altitudes where ultraviolet light, the part of the spectrum that burns, is stronger. Brimmed hats are likewise important.

Lips can suffer from windburn as well as sunburn, so a tube of lip balm can save you from days of pain.

11

First Aid and Emergencies

T HE CHANCES OF INFLICTING more than a scratch or two upon yourself on a canoe trip are remote. Driving to and from your destination is clearly more dangerous than the canoe trip itself. Still, a little preparation in matters related to first aid and emergencies is always in order. This kind of situation is almost certain never to happen, but you'll want to be prepared if it does.

HYPOTHERMIA

It's a cold day of camping: Do *you* have hypothermia? According to Dr. James Wilkerson, author of *Medicine for Mountaineering,* "Early signs may be undue fatigue, weakness, slowness of gait, apathy, forgetfulness, and confusion. These symptoms must not be negligently ascribed to fatigue or altitude. In hypothermia, shivering may not occur, especially during heavy physical activity."

Hypothermia is an imposing term, but the condition it represents is simple—a lowering of the body's temperature to a dangerous level. Any camper exposed to cold weather can become a victim (contrary to popular opinion, hypothermia can occur even without your getting wet).

Once the body is chilled, the brain automatically begins to conserve body heat by constricting blood vessels in the arms and legs. Shivering begins as the body uses whatever energy is available to quickly generate heat. Then the body's core temperature begins to drop. As it falls below 95 degrees, there is difficulty with speech. Further decreases bring on muscle stiffness, irrational thinking, amnesia, and unconsciousness. Below a core temperature of 78 degrees lies death.

Dr. Wilkerson makes the case for being alert to the possibility of hypothermia: "Awareness of the causes of hypothermia and the rapidity with which fatal hypothermia can develop is the most important aspect of prevention."

Treatment of hypothermia is fairly simple—but the sooner, the better. Replace wet clothes with dry ones, and move the victim into a warm shelter. If the victim is unable to generate his or her own body heat, then heat from a supplemental source should be provided: If it's impossible to build a fire, body heat from others (lightly clothed for best results) is useful. Hot liquids may help, but *never* give the victim alcoholic drinks (they dilate the blood vessels, allowing even greater heat loss). If the victim becomes unconscious, the situation is extremely serious, and hospitalization is necessary as soon as possible.

Hypothermia can be prevented, to a large extent, if you wear adequate clothing, get proper food, and maintain good physical conditioning. The food you eat is important: Sugar and carbohydrates are quickly oxidized by the body to provide heat and energy. Another precaution against hypothermia is a strong cardiovascular system, so it pays to stay in good shape.

HEAT EXHAUSTION

Heat can be dangerous, too. The opposite of hypothermia is heat exhaustion, which occurs when the body cannot shed excess heat. This can be caused by high temperatures, especially if accompanied by high humidity, and the typical symptoms include faintness, rapid heart rate, nausea, and a cold, clammy skin. Heat is removed from the skin in the form of moisture, and if you're severely dehydrated, you can't sweat. The main way to prevent heat exhaustion is to drink plenty of water, much more than you think. If you still start to feel faint, stop and rest in the shade. If you feel dizzy or weak, lie down and drink as much water as possible.

MEDICAL AID

Taking a Red Cross, YMCA, or other first-aid course is always a good idea. There are many books on the subject; recommended ones include *Medicine for Mountaineering,* by James A. Wilkerson, and *The Outward Bound Wilderness First-Aid Handbook,* by Jeffrey Isaac and Peter Goth.

First-aid basics consist of a little knowledge and a few medical supplies. Outdoor stores usually sell a number of prepackaged first-aid kits, though their quality varies widely. You can also put your own together by browsing the shelves of your local drugstore (for the contents of a typical first-aid kit, see the checklist in the appendices).

On long trips into remote backcountry, you should also consider bringing wide-range antibiotics in case of illness or infection. Large groups need to carry larger, more comprehensive kits, with items such as inflatable splints.

SIGNALING

If you're injured or become seriously ill, you may have to alert others. In most remote areas, initial searches are made by air, so you need to be seen from above. A fire might create enough smoke to attract attention, but flares are quicker and more effective. Carrying several small flares makes more sense.

The alternative to flares is a strobe light. A number of models are available; one sends out a flash every second that is visible for three miles and is powered by a D-sized battery.

Mirrors can be used for signaling, though obviously only in sunlight. Any shiny object, such as aluminum foil or a camera lens, can be used in a pinch. Smoke and flares are more effective. If you're in open terrain and have no other signal devices, spreading out brightly colored pieces of gear could help rescuers locate you. Always carry at least one yellow or orange item for this purpose.

RESCUE PROCEDURES

In popular areas, attracting attention shouldn't be too difficult, but in wilderness areas, you may be dependent on others to report you missing. For this reason, you always should leave word with someone as to where you're going and when you'll be back, especially if you're going alone. The route details you leave should be precise.

If you're in a group, someone can be sent for help if the group can't manage to go together. It's important that whoever goes has all the necessary information: the location of the injured person, the time of the accident, a description of the injuries, and the size and experience of the group. This information should be written down so that important details aren't forgotten under the stress of the moment.

SURVIVAL

A number of items may prove helpful to those undertaking a long trip in remote areas. On such a journey, it's always a good idea to take extra food, just in case you become stranded due to weather or if the trip takes longer than you expected. A good supply of high-energy bars is recommended. Emergency space blankets, which reflect and retain body heat, may prove useful. For detailed information on survival techniques, read *Practical Outdoor Survival: A Modern Approach*, by Len McDougall.

Saving Our Rivers

THE ENVIRONMENTAL PROTECTION AGENCY once tried to tally the number of dams on America's rivers, and it lost count at somewhere around sixty thousand. Over the years, dams have become integral to our way of life: They create power, divert water to our fields, and guard against the ravages of flood and drought. But in our rush to reap the benefits, some six hundred thousand miles of rivers have been drowned behind gates of concrete and steel.

Only recently have we become concerned with the fate of our rivers. The National Wild and Scenic Rivers Act was enacted to highlight the importance of rivers over dams. How well has it worked? There are now over ten thousand miles of rivers protected by the National Wild and Scenic Rivers System. This number sounds impressive, but unfortunately, it's not even one-half of 1 percent of America's rivers. For each mile of river preserved, eighty-five miles have been lost to dams.

But consider the alternative were the Act not in place. There have been many significant achievements, and with the efforts of canoeists like you, the future looks very bright indeed.

WILD AND SCENIC

What's needed, said Congress, is a law to counterbalance the national agenda encouraging dams. All that remained was to set down the details of the Act, but that process, as usual, took years. In 1968 the Act was finally passed, along with its policy that certain rivers possess such outstanding attributes of scenery, recreation, geology, fish, wildlife, history, and culture that they be preserved—free-flowing for all time.

There's nothing complex about the Act. It protects rivers by classifying them as wild, scenic, or recreational. It's a form of zoning, but instead of resolving disputes about urban sprawl, it focuses on sustaining the wildness of the backcountry.

But the classifications, however important, are secondary to the real purpose of the Act—to stop dams. The Act goes even further, by allowing managers to control development of the river corridor, either through outright purchase or through scenic easements.

Initially, sections of eight rivers were protected: the Rogue, the Middle Fork of the Salmon, the Clearwater, the Rio Grande, the Wolf, the St. Croix, the Eleven Point, and the Feather. In the first ten years of the Act, only eight more rivers were included.

A 1978 report of the comptroller general concluded that progress had been "excessively slow and costly." Two reasons were given: (1) federal agencies were taking too much time (an average of six and a half years) to assess a river's eligibility, and (2) states were not acting on their own because of high costs. The report said the process had become costly because of private land speculation (a four-year delay on Washington's Skagit caused an increase from $520 to $2,670 an acre).

Other problems exist. The Act is powerless to prevent dams upstream unless they "unreasonably diminish" the values of the river. A dam upstream may reduce flows to such a level that the resulting trickle can hardly be called a river. An example is the Little Miami River in Ohio, where dams on the unprotected Ash Fork and Caesar Creek tributaries alter the flow by some 30 percent.

Another misconception is that the Act prohibits dams in wilderness areas. Unfortunately, an agency can overrule the wilderness designation and allow a dam. A case in point is Glen Canyon Dam on the Colorado, which flooded Rainbow Bridge National Monument. A dam in the Grand Canyon—a national park, but not part of the Wild and Scenic Rivers System—is still a possibility.

The Act came too late for a number of outstanding rivers, and the river fatalities are startling. Entire river systems have fallen prey: The Tennessee River Valley has more miles of reservoir shoreline than all five Great Lakes. All but 149 miles of the 2,446 miles of the Missouri River have been dammed, and that 149-mile section would have been too if it hadn't been included in the Act.

The Colorado River has been impounded to such an extent that, with the exception of local floods, none of its water has reached the Pacific in twenty-five years. The Columbia has been reduced to a succession of reservoirs, with little moving water in between them.

Almost all the free-flowing rivers of California's Sierras are shells of their former selves. A magnificent stretch of the Dolores in Colorado has been sacrificed in the name of irrigation water so expensive no farmer can afford it. Glen Canyon, perhaps the most beautiful sandstone labyrinths in the world, now lies underneath

Lake Powell, where you'd need scuba equipment to enjoy it. And the list goes on.

DAM DECISIONS

How does this happen? The machinations by which dams are built are a study in pork-barrel politics. Most water projects are approved on the basis of a theoretical study called a cost-benefit analysis. Its name is imposing, but the actual procedure is relatively simple.

The first step is an estimation of the project's installation and operating *costs*. Then the *benefits* are estimated from the goods and services that will be produced. Next calculated are the secondary costs and benefits.

The analysis sounds so objective, how could anyone find fault with it? The procedure is considerably more subjective than you might imagine, given how agencies determine what constitutes costs and benefits. The deciding agencies are usually involved in construction, and there's evidence that they are biased. The courts have found that they often exaggerate benefits or underestimate costs in order to justify construction.

Flat-water recreation is commonly used to promote dams, but losses of streamside recreation are frequently ignored. Often neglected are environmental damages, such as flooding of historical and archaeological sites. Not to mention the consequences to fish and wildlife caused by changing water temperatures, increased salinity, and elimination of natural beaches. After all, cost-benefit is economics, and the procedure requires conversion into monetary terms. Dollar amounts must be placed on the environment, but what price do you put on the aesthetic and ecological advantages of a free-flowing stream? Or its loss?

The most important players in the game are the Army Corps of Engineers, the Bureau of Reclamation, and the Tennessee Valley Authority. Monetary benefits from flat-water recreation are usually touted by these agencies, even if other nearby reservoirs are being underused. Rarely is the destruction of fast-water recreation considered a cost, though lost revenues from these activities can substantially affect an economy.

Dams are often built so that development can move in, making another dam necessary to protect the development encouraged by the first, and so on. The Cossatot River in Arkansas's Ouachita Mountains is a good example. Gillham Dam was justified (75 percent of its benefits) because of damage it would prevent in floods. Yet the area below the dam had little on it to protect: a few barns, a shack or two, a handful of gravel roads, and a pasture with several hundred head of cattle. It would have been much cheaper to purchase the entire floodplain. There had never been a flood death on the Cossatot, but the dam was built.

Hydroelectric benefits are claimed, even if power isn't needed. The Alaska Power Authority proposed dams on the Susitna and other rivers, though it didn't have any contracts with utility companies. The reason was simple: It was cheaper to use oil and gas for power. Dam developers receive not only subsidies, but guaranteed markets, and it's no coincidence that demand for electricity is nowhere near that projected.

Irrigation, too, is used to justify dams. Cheap water encourages agriculture, and the result is a substantial subsidy. Water that may have cost the government $70 to $100 an acre-foot to develop is often sold for as little as $3 or $4.

In the end, it may prove ironic that the most effective way of saving rivers is economics. If it can be shown that a project is inefficient, then the figures themselves may stop the project.

SUCCESSES

The Wild and Scenic Rivers Act had its watershed year in 1980, with the largest number of rivers added (a total of twenty-six), all of which were Alaskan. President Carter, who made no friends in the dam lobby when he threatened to put the Corps out of business, saw this as one of his greatest achievements.

With the election of Reagan as president, it was feared that progress would be stalled on a riverless plateau. But the Reagan administration was more amenable than expected, though not without some prodding. Numbers can't tell the whole story, but a tally is revealing. In the first four years, from 1981 to 1984, not one river was included. Eventually twenty-five rivers were added, almost all in 1987.

With the Bush administration, things improved considerably. The number of river segments protected almost doubled to the present total of 150 or so. Which brings the average number of rivers protected every year since 1968 to only six.

In the twenty-five-plus years since the ink dried on the Act, there have been notable successes—over ten thousand miles of rivers saved. But much remains to be done: A long list of rivers has been identified by Congress as potential additions, but the process is slow. As a result, the rate of river mileage lost is seventy-five times *greater* than the rate of river preservation.

Only a minority of states have programs to protect rivers. Even on state-protected rivers, the Federal Energy Regulatory Commission (FERC) can override the designation, making it imperative that those rivers eventually be added to the federal system.

In the meantime, several conservation groups are pursuing private pacts with federal agencies and corporations to buy time. The Nature Conservancy has spent millions of dollars to purchase lands for preservation along rivers. The organization called American Rivers has secured years of protection through agreements with the Forest Service and the forest products industry.

Then there's the old-fashioned appeal to the grassroots, as occurred in the mid-'60s when dams were proposed in the Grand Canyon. This prompted the Sierra Club to place full-page ads asking, "Should we flood the Sistine Chapel so tourists can get closer to the ceiling?" The response from the public, most of whom would never see the river, was so overwhelming that even the politicians got the message.

A dozen years later, another highly publicized debate arose over New Melones Dam on California's Stanislaus River. The controversy climaxed when a lanky lad named Mark Dubois chained himself to the riverbanks to stop further inundation. Preservation efforts were unsuccessful, but in the long run the river lobby won by bringing attention to saving our last remaining rivers.

THE FUTURE

Reflecting back on the work of the river conservation movement (John Muir lost the first major dam fight when he opposed Hetchy Dam in Yosemite), it's the cruelest of paradoxes that those who restore antiques and fine art are called philanthropists, while those who try to save the last of our rivers are labeled radicals.

Arguably, some dams do provide benefits that can't be obtained in other ways: irrigation, domestic water supplies, flood control, hydroelectric power. But where do we draw the line? Former Secretary of Interior Cecil Andrus argues that "Streams and rivers have other values than just for electric power generation and irrigation and transportation. We need free-flowing water left in the nation for many reasons—including the protection of certain forms of life, for recreation, for scenic values, for maintenance of the tenuous link between modern man and his natural world."

In his book *Time and the River Flowing*, François Leydet points out the dilemma: "I suppose if we accept as a national policy that every resource of the country must be developed to the limit to support the greatest possible human population, then we should right now give up the fight to save any untouched vestiges of our natural heritage. All rivers must be dammed, to prevent their wasting water into the ocean, and the consequent destruction of the beauty of natural rivers must be shrugged off as one of the prices of progress."

If we decide, instead, that rivers are worth saving, then the political field must be leveled. Before another dam is built, its benefits should be proven so overwhelming that no other reasonable alternative exists. It's only right that the burden be placed on those advocating change, not those supporting the status quo—a river in its natural state.

Otherwise, the consequences for all of us are too great to ignore. Because no force of nature affects the human spirit quite like running water. And with few exceptions, no amount of progress can be worth the loss of a river flowing free.

Appendices

Checklists

Checklists are essential. Make lists of everything you'll need on the trip, organizing them according to categories: boating equipment, kitchen box, personal gear, first-aid kit, survival kit, repair kit, and human-waste-disposal equipment. The following are only suggestions—make your own to fit your specific needs and preferences.

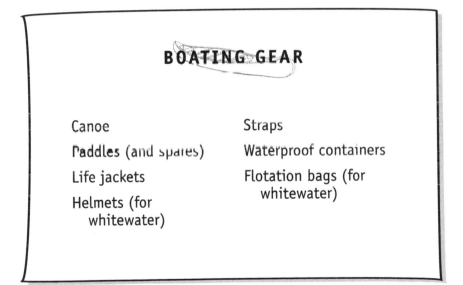

BOATING GEAR

Canoe

Paddles (and spares)

Life jackets

Helmets (for whitewater)

Straps

Waterproof containers

Flotation bags (for whitewater)

KITCHEN BOX

Pots and pans

Eating utensils

Long spoon (for stirring)

Can opener

Drinking cups

Waters containers

Camping stove and fuel

Grill

Firepan

Dutch oven

Charcoal briquettes

Knife

Matches (or other fire starter)

Plates

Ax, shovel, saw

Biodegradable dishwashing soap

Aluminum foil

Paper towels

Plastic bags with fasteners

Pot-gripper pliers

Pot scrubber

Dishwashing buckets

Water purification disinfectants (chlorine and iodine)

Water filtering device

Salt, pepper, other spices

Sugar, flour

CAMPING GEAR

Tent (with poles, stakes)

Tarp

Sleeping bag

Sleeping pad

Lantern

PERSONAL GEAR

Clothing

Shirts

Shorts

Long pants

Sweater—pile/fleece

Bandanna

Underwear

Belt

Hat

Gloves

Insulated jacket

Long underwear

Rain jacket and pants

Shoes

Socks

Swimsuit

Dirty clothes bag

Other

Flashlight (with spare
batteries, bulbs)

Biodegradable hand
soap, shampoo

Sunglasses

Suntan lotion

Lip balm

Towel

Toothbrush, toothpaste

Toilet paper

Mosquito repellent

Nylon line (clothes
drying, repairs, etc.)

Needles and thread

Camera

Fishing gear

Binoculars

Knife

FIRST-AID KIT

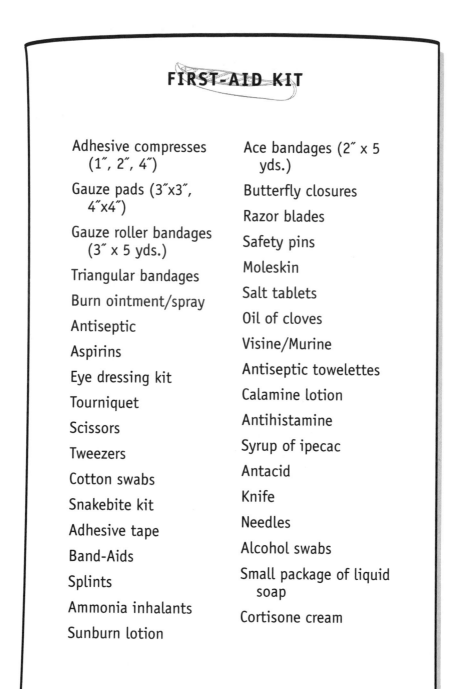

- Adhesive compresses (1″, 2″, 4″)
- Gauze pads (3″x3″, 4″x4″)
- Gauze roller bandages (3″ x 5 yds.)
- Triangular bandages
- Burn ointment/spray
- Antiseptic
- Aspirins
- Eye dressing kit
- Tourniquet
- Scissors
- Tweezers
- Cotton swabs
- Snakebite kit
- Adhesive tape
- Band-Aids
- Splints
- Ammonia inhalants
- Sunburn lotion
- Ace bandages (2″ x 5 yds.)
- Butterfly closures
- Razor blades
- Safety pins
- Moleskin
- Salt tablets
- Oil of cloves
- Visine/Murine
- Antiseptic towelettes
- Calamine lotion
- Antihistamine
- Syrup of ipecac
- Antacid
- Knife
- Needles
- Alcohol swabs
- Small package of liquid soap
- Cortisone cream

SURVIVAL KIT

Signal mirror

Flares

Whistle

Candles

Fire starter/waterproof
matches

Nylon cord (20´)

Space blanket

Dextrose cubes

Energy bars

REPAIR KIT

Duct tape

Patching material and
adhesive

Repair tools (as
appropriate)

Pliers

Epoxy glue

Bailing wire

Spare parts

HUMAN-WASTE-DISPOSAL EQUIPMENT

Surplus ammo box

Toilet seat

Deodorant chemical
(dry lime, AquaChem,
or chlorine)

Toilet paper

Water dispenser

Hand soap

Recommended Reading

Allan, Melinda. *Canoeing Basics.* New York: Hearst Marine Books, 1994.

Bechdel, Les, and Slim Ray. *River Rescue.* Boston: Appalachian Mountain Club, 1989.

Harrison, Dave. *Canoeing: The Complete Guide to Equipment and Technique.* Mechanicsburg, PA: Stackpole Books, 1995.

Jacobson, Cliff. *Canoeing Wild Rivers.* Merrillville, IN: ICS Books, Inc., 1984.

Landry, Paul, and Mattie McNair. *The Outward Bound Canoeing Handbook.* New York: Lyons & Burford, 1992.

Mason, Bill. *Path of the Paddle.* Minocqua, WI: Northword Press, 1980.

Mason, Bill. *Song of the Paddle: An Illustrated Guide to Wilderness Camping.* Minocqua, WI: Northword Press, 1988.

Ray, Slim. *The Canoe Handbook: Techniques for Mastering the Sport of Canoeing.* Mechanicsburg, PA: Stackpole Books, 1992.

Walbridge, Charles, and Wayne Sundmacher. *Whitewater Rescue Manual.* Camden, ME: Ragged Mountain Press, 1995.

Useful Addresses

Canoe Camping Supplies

L. L. Bean, Inc.
Freeport, ME 04033
800/221-4221

Duluth Tent & Awning, Inc.
P.O. Box 16024
Duluth, MN 55816-0024
800/777-4439

NOC Outfitter's Store
13077 Hwy. 19 W.
Bryson City, NC 28713-9114
800/367-3521

Piragis Northwoods Company
105 North Central Ave.
Ely, MN 55731
800/223-6565

Recreational Equipment, Inc.
1700 45th St. E.
Sumner, WA 98390
800/426-4840

Associations

American Canoe Association
(ACA)
7432 Alban Station Rd.
Suite B-226
Springfield, VA 22150
703/451-0141

American Rivers
801 Pennsylvania Ave. S.E.
Suite 400
Washington, DC 20003
202/547-6900

United States Canoe Association
606 Ross St.
Middletown, OH 45044
513/422-3739

Canoe Manufacturers

American Traders Classic Canoes
627 Barton Rd.
Greenfield, MA 01301
413/773-9631

Atkinson Boat Co.
3258 E. Mullett Lake Rd.
Indiana River, MI 49749
616/238-8825

Bear Creek Canoe, Inc.
RR 1, Box 1638, Rt. 11
Limerick, ME 04048
207/793-2005
Fax 207/793-4733

Bell Canoe Works
25355 Hwy. 169 S.
Zimmerman, MN 55398
612/856-2231

Black Duck Boat Shop
143 West St.
New Milford, CT 06776
203/350-5170 #3

Blackhawk Canoe
1140 North Parker Dr.
Jonesville, WI 53545
608/754-2179

Bluegrass Canoes, Inc.
7323 Peaks Mill Rd.
Frankfort, KY 40601
502/227-4492
Fax 502/227-8086

Blue Hole Canoe Company
18079-B James Madison Hwy.
Gordonsville, VA 22942
540/832-7855
Fax 540/832-7854

Bluewater Canoes/
Rockwood Outfitters
699 Speedvale Ave. W.
Guelph, ON N1K 1E6, Canada
519/824-1415
Fax 519/824-8750

Bourquin Boats
1568 McMahon Blvd.
Ely, MN 55731
218/365-5499

Bryan Boatbuilding
RR 3, St. George
NB, E0G 2Y0, Canada
506/755-2486

Burt's Canoes
Rt. 1, Box 1090
Litchfield, ME 04350
207/268-4802

Cal-Tek Engineering
36 Riverside Dr.
Kingston, MA 02364
617/585-5666

Camp Canoes
9 Averill
Otego, NY 13825
607/988-6842

Canoes by Whitewell Ltd.
2362 Dresden Dr.
Atlanta, GA 30341
404/325-5330

Cedarwood Canoes
Port Sanfield, RR 2
Port Carling, ON P0B 1J0, Canada
705/765-6282

Chamcock Boat & Canoe
Glebe Rd., RR 2
St. Andrews, NB E0G 2X0, Canada
506/529-4776

Chicagoland Canoe Base, Inc.
4109 N. Narragansett Ave.
Chicago, IL 60634
312/777-1489

Curtis Canoe, Inc.
P. O. Box 750
Honeoye, NY 14471
715/229-5022
Fax 716/229-4723

Dagger Canoe Co.
P. O. Box 1500
Harriman, TN 37748
615/882-0404
Fax 615/882-8153

Dagger Composites
315 Roddy Ln.
Harriman, TN 37748
615/882-3547
Fax 615/882-8317

Easy Rider Canoe & Kayak Co.
P. O. Box 88108
Seattle, WA 98138
206/228-3633

Englehart Products, Inc.
P. O. Box 377
Newbury, OH 44065
216/564-5565
Fax 216/564-5515

Explorer Canoe Co.
P. O. Box 173
Lyndonville, VT 05851
802/626-8648
Fax 802/626-1157

Fletcher Canoes
Hwy. 11B, Box #1321
Aikokan, ON P0T 1C0, Canada
807/597-6801

Grasse River Boatworks
P. O. Box 496
Canton, NY 13617
315/386-1363

Great Canadian Canoe Co.
64 Worcester Providence Tpke.
(Rt. 146)
Sutton, MA 01590
508/865-0010

Grumman Canoes/OMC Aluminum Boat Group
P. O. Box 549
Marathon, NY 13803
607/849-3211

Hemlock Canoe Works
P. O. Box 68
Hemlock, NY 14466-0068
716/367-3040

Hoefgen Canoes
N1927/Hwy. M-35
Menominee, MI 49858
906/863-3991

Indian River Canoe Mfg.
4155 South St.
Titusville, FL 32780
407/267-7575

Jensen Canoes Research
308 78th Ave. N.
Minneapolis, MN 55444
612/561-2229
473 N. Robin Hood Rd.
Inverness, FL 33450
904/344-0624

Karel Fiberglass Products
789 Kailua Rd.
Kailua, HI 96734
808/261-8626
Fax 808/261-8424

Kevin Martin, Boatbuilder
RFD 1, Box 441
Epping, NH 03042
603/679-5153

Kruger Ventures
2906 Meister Lane
Lansing, MI 48906
517/323-2139

Leisure Life Ltd.
4855 Broadmoor S.E.
Grand Rapids, MI 49512
616/698-3000
616/698-2734

Lincoln PaddleLite Canoes
RR 2, Box 106
Freeport, ME 04032
207/865-0455

Mad River Canoe
P. O. Box 610
Waitsfield, VT 05673
802/496-3127
Fax 802/496 6247

Massive Outdoor Products
100 Hinchey Ave., Suite 517
Ottawa, ON K1Y 4L9, Canada
613/728-7931

McCurdy & Reed Canoes
RR 2, Hampton Annapolis
NS B0S 1L0, Canada
902/665-2435

Merrimack Canoe Co., Inc.
202 Harper Ave.
Crossville, TN 38555
615/484-4556
Fax 615/456-7918

Meyers Boat Co.
343 Lawrence St.
Adrian, MI 49221
517/265-9821

Mid-Canada Fiberglass Ltd./ Scott
Canoe Co.
Box 1599
New Liskeard, ON P0J 1P0
Canada
705/647-6548
Fax 705/647-6698

Middle Path Boats
Box 8881
Pittsburgh, PA 15221
412/247-4860

Millbrook Boats
49 Lufkin Rd.
Weare, NH 03281
603/529-3919

Miller Canoes
RR 1 Nictou
Plaster Rock, NB E0J 1W0,
Canada
506/356-2409
Fax 506/356-2409

Mohawk Canoes
963 N CR 427
Longwood, FL 32750
407/834-3233
Fax 407/834-0292

Monfort Associates
RR 2, Box 416
Wiscasset, ME 04578-9610
207/882-5504

Moore Canoes
3 Cardinal Court
Hilton Head Island, SC 29926
803/681-5986

Marley Cedar Canoes
P. O. Box 5147
Swan Lake, MT 59911
406/886-2242

Muskoka Fine Watercraft &
Supply Co. Ltd.
24 Brock St. W.
Uxbridge, ON L9P 1P3, Canada
905/731-8295
Fax 905/731-0197

Nature Bound Canoe
Rt. 140, 93 Gardner Rd.
Winchendon, MA 01475
508/297-0288

Navarro Canoe Co.
199 Rogue River Pkwy.
Talent, OR 97540
503/482-8095

New River Canoe Mfg., Inc.
Rt. 2, Box 575
Independence, VA 24348
703/773-3124

Nova Craft Canoes Ltd.
4389 Exeter Rd.
London, ON N6L 1A4, Canada
519/652-3649
Fax 519/762-6803

Old Town Canoe Co.
38 Middle St.
Old Town, ME 04468
207/827-5513
Fax 207/827-2779

Pakboats
P. O. Box 700
Enfield, NH 03748
603/632-7654
Fax 603/632-5611

Patrick Moore Canoeing
P. O. Box 242
Stoughton, WI 53589
608/873-5989

Phoenix Products, Inc.
P. O. Box 109
207 North Broadway
Berea, KY 40403
606/986-2336
Fax 606/986-3277

Porta-Bote International
1074 Independence Ave.
Mountain View, CA 94043
800/227-8882

Prijon/Wildwasser Sport USA,
Inc.
P. O. Box 4671
Boulder, CO 80306
303/444-2336
Fax 303/444-2375

Radisson Products
P. O. Box 130
Callander, ON P0H 1H0, Canada
705/752-3660

Red River Canoe & Paddle
63 Ellesmere Ave.
Winnepeg, MB R2M 0G4, Canada
204/231-1872

Riverjammer Canoe Co.
191 Crawley Falls Rd
Brentwood, NH 03833
Phone and fax 603/642-8522

Ruch Canoes
Minett Post Office
Muskoka, ON P0B 1G0, Canada
705/765-5390 or -3588

Sawyer Canoe Co.
234 S. State St.
Oscola, MI 48750
517/739-9181

Souris River Canoes
104 Reid St., Box 1116
Atikokan, ON P0T 1C0, Canada
807/597-1292
Fax 807/597-5871

Spencer Canoes
Rt. 1, Box 55R
Martindale, TX 78655
512/357-6113

Stewart River Boatworks
Rt. 1, Box 2038
Two Harbors, MN 55616
218/834-5037

Swift Canoe & Kayak Co.
RR 1, Oxtongue Lake
Dwight, ON P0A 1H0, Canada
705/635-1167
Fax 705/635-1834

Temagami Canoe Co.
P. O. Box 520
Temagami, ON P0H 2H0, Canada
705/569-3777

Tender Craft Boat Shop, Inc.
284 Brock Ave.
Toronto, ON MK6 2M4, Canada
416/531 2941
Fax 416/323-0992

Three Rivers Canoe Co.
P. O. Box 173
Lyndonville, VT 05851
802/626-8648
Fax 802/626-1157

Trailhead
1960 Scott St.
Ottawa, ON K1Z 8L8, Canada
613/722-4229
Fax 613/722-0245

Vermont Canoe Products
RR 1, Box 353A
Newport, VT 05855
Phone and fax 802/754-2307

We-no-nah Canoe, Inc.
P. O. Box 247
Winona, MN 55987
507/454-5430
Fax 507/454-5448

West Coast Canoe Co.
P. O. Box 143
Campbell River, BC V9W 5A7,
Canada
800/446-1588

Western Canoeing Mfg., Inc.
Box 115
Abbotsford, BC V2S 4N8, Canada
604/853-9320
Fax 604/852-6933

Woodstrip Watercraft Co.
1818 Swamp Pike
Gilbertsville, PA 19525
610/326-9282

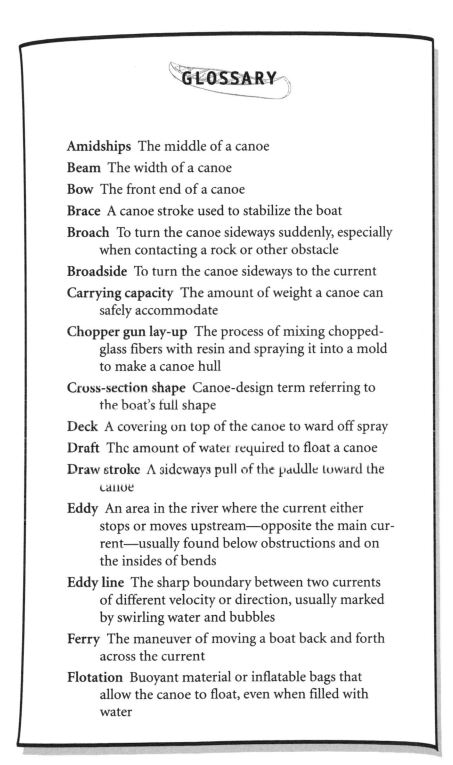

GLOSSARY

Amidships The middle of a canoe

Beam The width of a canoe

Bow The front end of a canoe

Brace A canoe stroke used to stabilize the boat

Broach To turn the canoe sideways suddenly, especially when contacting a rock or other obstacle

Broadside To turn the canoe sideways to the current

Carrying capacity The amount of weight a canoe can safely accommodate

Chopper gun lay-up The process of mixing chopped-glass fibers with resin and spraying it into a mold to make a canoe hull

Cross-section shape Canoe-design term referring to the boat's full shape

Deck A covering on top of the canoe to ward off spray

Draft The amount of water required to float a canoe

Draw stroke A sideways pull of the paddle toward the canoe

Eddy An area in the river where the current either stops or moves upstream—opposite the main current—usually found below obstructions and on the insides of bends

Eddy line The sharp boundary between two currents of different velocity or direction, usually marked by swirling water and bubbles

Ferry The maneuver of moving a boat back and forth across the current

Flotation Buoyant material or inflatable bags that allow the canoe to float, even when filled with water

Freeboard The measurement from the waterline of a canoe to the top of the gunwales, used to determine if a canoe is overloaded

Gradient The slope of a riverbed, usually expressed in the number of feet per mile the river drops

Gunwales The railings around the outer rim of the canoe

Hard chines Sharp, nearly right-angle edges where the bottom and the sides of the canoe meet

Hole A reversal (see below)

Hull The basic shell of the canoe

Initial stability A canoe's resistance to tipping when first entered or subjected to waves

Keel line The ridge on the canoe's bottom extending from bow to stern, allowing the boat to track (or stay on course) better

Leeward Toward a sheltered area out of the wind

Lining The process of guiding the canoe from the shore with ropes to avoid rapids or other hazards

Livery A canoe rental shop

Painter A line (usually short) attached to the bow or stern of a canoe for securing it to the shore

PFD A Personal Flotation Device, or life jacket

Pivot To turn sharply

Portage To carry boats and equipment around rapids by way of the shore

Pry stroke A sideways push of the paddle away from the canoe

Reversal An area of the river where the current turns upstream and revolves back on itself, forming a treacherous current requiring caution; often called hydraulics, stoppers, keepers, curlers, and holes

Ribs Curved supports inside some canoes that add rigidity and structural strength

Rocker The amount of upward curve on a canoe's hull; the more rocker, the quicker the boat will pivot

Scout To examine a rapid from shore

Secondary stability A canoe's resistance to tipping in heavy waves; usually best in more rounded hulls

Sheer line The curvature of the canoe between the bow and the stern

Shuttle Transportation between the beginning and ending points of a canoe trip

Skid plate A layer of extra material applied to the underside of the bow to aid in resisting abrasion

Soft chines A gradual curve where the bottom and the sides of the canoe meet

Splash cover A fabric cover that fits over the top of the canoe to keep out spray

Standing wave A high wave caused by the slowing of the current

Stern The rear of a canoe

Strainer Exposed rocks, usually on the outside of a bend, that present a hazard to boaters

Swamp To fill the canoe with water

Sweeper Fallen trees or brush that lie in the path of the current

Tandem A canoe built for two paddlers sitting in the bow and stern

Throw bag A bag stuffed with rope to be thrown for use in river rescues

Thwart A cross-brace on a canoe used for structural integrity

Tongue The smooth V of fast water found at the head of rapids, usually indicating the deepest and least-obstructed channel

Thwart A cross-beam on a canoe

Track To move the canoe in a straight line

Trim A canoe's balance when in the water

Tumblehome An inward curving of a canoe's sides above the waterline

Yoke A special frame designed to aid in carrying the canoe on one's shoulders during a portage

Index